AF247513

ILLUSIONS
OF
SUCCESS

ILLUSIONS OF SUCCESS

John Curtis Raines

JUDSON PRESS, VALLEY FORGE

ILLUSIONS OF SUCCESS

Copyright © 1975
Judson Press, Valley Forge, PA 19481

Library of Congress Cataloging in Pubication Data

Raines, John C.
    Illusions of success.

    Includes bibliographical references and index.
    1. Middle classes—United States.   2. Social mobility—United States.
3. Wealth—United States.   4. Cost and standard of living—United States.
I. Title.
HT690.U6R34   301.44′1   74-22525
ISBN 0-8170-0650-8

Printed in the U.S.A.

To Bonnie

ACKNOWLEDGMENTS

I acknowledge with gratitude permission to use substantial portions of my articles, "Middle Class: Up Against the Wall and Going Nowhere" and "Middle Class Incentive for Change," reprinted from the May 3, 1973, and September 4-11, 1974, issues of *The Christian Century*. Also, I am grateful to *Christianity and Crisis* for allowing me to use major portions of my article "The Middle Class: Unmasking the American Myth," printed in their April 15, 1974, issue.

I want to thank Peter Bachrach, James Kuhn, Ben Bagdikian, Roger Shinn, Joseph Margolis, and Glenn Jacobson for reading portions or all of this manuscript and for giving in other ways valuable criticism and suggestions along the way of its inception and completion. I am, of course, alone responsible for the final form and point of view expressed in these pages.

Sharon Ramey, Linda Anderson, Joselyn Dibaee, and Nancy Hall, of the Department of Religion at Temple University, helped in typing the manuscript and toiled diligently with my cribbed handwriting and not always dependable spelling. John Luetzow prepared the index.

Finally, I would be remiss in accounting my gratitudes if I did not mention the amazingly diverse student body of Temple University without whose insistent instruction and determined dignity I would not, I believe, have turned my attention to the hope and hurt of the American middle class and those who aspire thereto.

CONTENTS

Affluence, upward mobility, and freedom of opportunity are American dreams that do more to disguise than to reveal American realities. What we have believed about ourselves in the past makes increasingly less sense out of what is happening to us today. We are not middle, and we are not mobile, nor do we enjoy much affluence. Rather than a *middle*-class society, we are a society of wage earners and wealth owners with very little movement between the two groups. Rather than experiencing upward mobility, we feel as if we were caught in a stampede and were stumbling over hidden roadblocks. Statistics show that this feeling has an astonishingly accurate relationship to reality. Moreover, we are living not so much in affluence but by middle-class moonlighting and end-of-the-week exhaustion.

To demonstrate this assertion, I will examine the living situation of average middle Americans. I mean those whose family income falls between $11,000 and $17,000 a year. Actually, that is above the statistically average family, which in 1973 was located at the lower end of that scale. Still, the $10,000 to $20,000 group is the one to which most poorer Americans aspire and the bracket within which American amenities like affluence and upward mobility are thought to take hold—together with standard poor-mouthing of the middle class like consumerism and excessive materialism.

In fact, neither the amenities nor the denigrations describe what is going on—which is instead a combination of end-of-the-month desperation and misplaced gratitude. For we live in a society that is steeply unequal, where most of the effective (that is, discretionary) wealth and, therefore, power is frozen at the top. Yet this reality is disguised as right, good, and only natural by the myth of freedom of opportunity. If everyone has a "fair chance," then no one has a right to complain—except against himself.

Curiously, this myth buttresses itself upon the idea of free and universal education. I say curiously, because what education has shown itself best at, and statistically does most massively, is *failing* people at gaining status accomplishment—only three A's for every fifteen B's for every twenty-five C's, and so on. And an education in failure is less an education in freedom of opportunity than a tutoring in self-doubt and the redirecting of our social frustration and anger inward against ourselves in self-blame.

Still, I do not want to argue that most Americans have not bettered themselves since coming to these shores. We have, thanks to industrialization and a rapidly expanding Gross National Product. But this betterment in absolute terms has not been matched by much improvement in the relative scale. We have moved up. But those above us have moved up more. And since upward mobility is the way in which a middle-class people measures and judges itself as respectable, we can see the problem this lack of real mobility creates. While moving up in things, we have not moved up in spirit. In the final measuring we do not, most of us, really feel that our lives are successful.

Moreover—and this is key, the energy/raw material/pollution crisis promises to pinch off any rapid expansion of the overall economy in the future and so end the endless escalator. We just cannot make the pie bigger and bigger anymore. Consequently, the issue of how the pie gets sliced up—the distribution of wealth and advantages—becomes crucial.

Only in a more equal America can this slower economic growth rate be handled within the boundaries of democratic consent. For the removal of steep inequalities in our society is the single force that can change the dimensions of our personal and collective dreaming. We will more readily stop the panic running when there is not that far ahead to get, nor that far back to fall. Only a more equal America can cool the middle-class stampede into a (newly necessary) long-haul walk.

What we need then is a new vision of society beyond the buccaneer pursuit of success—a perhaps more modest but still Good Life, not ahead but *where we are,* and in reality rather than in our dreams. We also need a politics to make it real. My thesis is that this politics can be found in the vast American middle class. This group, too—and not just the traditional 20 to 25 percent underclass—suffers from a fundamental deprivation—an inequality of wealth, of political power, and of social status. To climb from the lower to the middle group in our society does not change this underlying fact, although it may change the number of times we eat meat each week.

More fundamentally, we need a more equal society not simply because of the necessities of a slowed economic growth rate, but to keep faith with the basic wager about the dignity of persons that is implied by our democratic experiment. Always true, but even more true today, democracy cannot long survive our continuing inequalities. The alternative is tyranny—survival imposed from above. We do not need to go that way, but without basic change, we will.

1 DREAMS

> "When little is known, or only trivial items publicized, or when myths prevail, then plain description becomes a radical fact—or at least is taken to be radically upsetting."[1]
>
> —C. Wright Mills

In the summer of 1972 a president of the United States said a very typical thing. "1972 was a good year," Richard Nixon said, "and 1973 will be a great one!" He was running for reelection. Actually, 1972–1973 was a year of steep inflation—so steep that only the highly benefited few managed to stay even with, much less get ahead of, the rising price index. Most of us were downwardly mobile that year and had been for several years before. According to government figures, the average income in the $10,000 to $25,000 bracket in 1970 was $15,500 and by 1973 had risen to an average $16,300. But relatively unnoticed, the actual purchasing power of this middle/upper middle-class income had in those three years *dropped* by $3,079.[2]

All this made 1972–73 a time to assess the progress of the American Dream with more than usual clarity. Why? Because it provided a moment of enforced skepticism in the midst of our long-distance running and dreaming. As a result, America may be closer to fundamental change today than at any time in the recent past. In 1966, 45 percent of us agreed with the statement "the rich get richer while the poor get poorer." By 1973, 76 percent agreed.[3] The sleeping giant which is our country's middle class is beginning to stir. It is starting to suspect that it is overtaxed, overworked, and underrepresented by its elected representatives. Moreover, it is beginning to suspect these burdens are imposed not to care for the poor but to finance the advantages of the wealthy. During the two-year period 1972–1974, corporate executive salaries averaged a 27 percent increase.

This tremor of doubt could signal a political earthquake. There has always been plenty of frustration in our society, and it has fueled a good deal of resentment. But usually the resentment gets dumped upon the blacks or Jews or long-haired hippies and other favorite scapegoats. Should this sense of being cheated—of somehow working hard all of your life and still not getting very far—begin to focus itself upon the established system of wealth and advantage, then real change becomes possible. It all depends on what the middle class decides to believe about itself.

But just here is where the problem comes, for this examination takes us into the fundamental myths by which we hold together as a people. And these myths have deeply to do with ideas of being middle and mobile. We hold on to these ideas so passionately because through them we try to make sense of ourselves as a people and, often enough, as individual persons.

The difficulty is that to be a *middle*-class people is to be a people always on the run. It is to receive our reality as an "in-between"— between those behind, whom we fear and from whom we flee, and those ahead whom we envy and seek to emulate. As a *middle*-class people, self-respect is never found where we are but always just ahead there, where (we hope) we are going. We are in danger, therefore, of identifying with the dreams beyond us and so voting against the place we really are.

But what can we do? We have to make sense of it all somehow. We have paid too many prices to be cavalier about our hopes.

Becoming Somebody

"What do you do?" is a key part of opening rituals at parties where strangers meet and try to interact. The question is central to the production of a well-performed conviviality because the answer to it *maps in the system of deference.* It tells us how to approach each other in mutually anticipated ways—to play the same game. "What do you do?" registers accomplishment in gaining pecuniary advantage. There is a special structure for professionals. Medical doctors, for example, require more deference than teachers; and among the former—at least in upper-middle-class society—psychiatrists require more prestige-recognition gestures than internists. Ministers, priests, and rabbis form a separate category. They are, to say it frankly, something of an embarrassment to the usual status-role playing.

So far, we have been speaking about the rites of male association. The system has been different for females. The talk among females mapping their way through the social landscape of a cocktail party has more likely turned to husbands and children. Their system of comparative merit—happy husband, healthy kids, competent housewife—plays an integral role in commercial advertising's attempt to manipulate her as a household buyer. In fact, however, more and more middle-class wives are having to go back to work. The freedom to take a job may be middle-class liberation, but it is increasingly a middle-class necessity. The reason has already appeared. It has to do with that mapping word, that social definition called *middle* class.

Middle becomes valuable, a significant place to be, only as it promises something ever above itself, or at least appears to itself to do so. In a land of freedom of opportunity if we are not moving up, then there is only one place to put the blame—on ourselves! This fearing and resenting those behind and humbling ourselves before those above serve to consolidate the system.

Are we moving up—or are we having to run faster just to stay in place? The figures indicate that after a ten-year period, between 1961 and 1971, the statistically average family's budget increased, after taxes and inflation, by $1,610. Every year since 1971 that average family has *lost purchasing power*. In 1972–1973, for example, the wholesale price index went up by what even an administrative official called an "unbelievable" 17.5 percent. Still, taking just the good years, the additional $1,610 amounted to about $135 per month or $33 a week. After ten years of work is that moving up?

The answer becomes clearer when we look at what has been happening in the wider society around this average family. Take just one typical instance—the move to the suburbs by Mr. Middle. Let us follow a family that used to live in South Philadelphia—an Italian neighborhood of two- and three-story row houses. Making it in

America has come to mean making it out of the city and into the suburbs. If you do not believe me, just look at the scene outside those windows in the magazine advertisements: there are green trees, not sidewalks.

In this move, the family left behind a three-to-six bedroom row house (basement finished over the years and paneled) mostly or wholly paid for and bought originally for $7,000. They sold it for $10,000, which they used as a down payment on a $30.000 suburban home (maximum three bedroom) with a dishwasher and their own tree outside the window. That meant a $20,000 mortgage added to the family budget. We shall not discuss whether they now have more or less square footage of living space. In turn over the twenty-five year life of their mortgage they will have to pay back a total of $60,000 (average). In one stroke the family has added $165 to their monthly budget—i.e., more than their total ten-year monthly increase. Besides, they have had to purchase a second car for father to get to work at a monthly cost, conservatively estimated, of $90 with installment payments, gasoline, and insurance. There can be no doubt about it. This family has discovered end-of-the-month blues.

"Well, the wife can go to work. And besides, we did it for the kids; so they could get a good education, go to college, and beat the system."

Wage Earners Versus Wealth Owners

Does it work—this beating the system? The statistics show that if you are a wage earner your chances of ever becoming a wealth owner are slim. The game of getting big money and keeping it is, in fact, to *shield* your income from the heavily taxed wage and salary category. This is shown in the following chart. It reveals the percentage of yearly income that is derived from wage and from property in various brackets.

Notice the sharp break at about $25,000, with the larger percentage of income moving rapidly into the business and property column. (That was in 1962, the most recent year for which these figures are available. Today the break would more likely come at $35,000.) The reason for this sharp break is the tax advantages that are available on interest, dividends, rentals, and so on.

Wage/Property Income[4]
(percentage relationship)

Annual Income	% from wages	% from business and property (interest, dividends, rents, etc.)
$ 0-2,999	41	14
3,000-4,999	72	13
5,000-7,499	84	11
7,500-9,999	85	12
10,000-14,999	84	14
15,000-24,999	78	20
25,000-49,999	47	51
50,000-99,999	38	61
over 100,000	17	82

One of the most important of these tax loopholes is "capital gains"—the tax on profits from the sale of corporate stocks and bonds. Only 50 percent of this income is even subject to tax. Then there is the tax-free interest on state and municipal bonds. The effect of all this can be seen in the following chart.[5]

a family of four with an income of $10,000 derived from—	pays in federal income tax—
wages and salary	$905.00
capital gains	98.00
state and municipal bonds	0.00

These loopholes have been justified on the grounds that they provide the risk capital which fuels a free economy. As one angry defender of the system put it to me, "You'll kill the goose that lays the golden egg!" To which I replied, "It's not my egg; and besides you've got the wrong goose." The truth is that American corporations in the 1960s derived only 1.5 percent of their reinvestment capital from the sale of stocks; 98.5 percent of their capital needs is met from withheld earnings, borrowings, and the like.[6]

A few of us, a very few, have become spectacularly successful at this game of sheltering our income from the heavily taxed wage and salary category. In 1972, according to a University of Michigan survey, 10 percent of our nation owned 56 percent of all the personally owned wealth.[7] In 1969 the top 1/2 of 1 percent of our population owned (note it well) fully half of that 56 percent, or 28 percent of the total wealth![8] This distribution of wealth has not changed significantly in our lifetime.

Moreover, remember Mr. Middle and his second car and newly acquired big mortgage. His $30,000 house and his two cars all get factored into the general wealth statistics. That is why we must introduce a key distinction between income-*producing* wealth and those financially static amenities that nevertheless get counted as "wealth" in economic surveys and Gross National Product figures.

Looking to wealth-producing wealth, we find a startling scene— startling, that is, for a land that prizes itself as a place of freedom of opportunity. In a landmark study in 1953, the economist R. J. Lampman found that more than 30 percent of the assets and equities in our society were held by 1.6 percent of our adult population (with another 20 percent held by government). This 1.6 percent, for example, held *all* state and local bonds (tax exempt) and 82 percent of all corporate stocks with their capital gains tax advantage.[9]

That leaves the rest of us (98.4 percent) to divide up the remaining 50 percent of the total assets and equities—"wealth" that is for the most part fully exposed to taxation: wages, cash savings, houses, cars, etc. As Peter Barnes put it in *The New Republic:*

> The great GNP machine has been moderately successful in distributing what might be called inert wealth—homes, automobiles, personal property—which, far from producing income, are a drain on the sturdiest pocketbook.[10]

The middle-class stampede takes most of us into a traffic jam—a traffic jam that ends in a roadblock.

What we need today is not more expansion of the economy but a redistribution of the wealth—taking the wealthy off tax welfare. If you do not believe me, contemplate the amount of concentrated power revealed in the following chart. It shows where wealth begins to *take off* in our society, the kind of wealth, that is, that can be translated into behind-the-scenes social control.[11]

We should notice two things about these figures. First is the striking reality that those who really make it in America take their steep rise only above $50,000 a year, where tax breaks start going up in multiples of 3, then 4, and at last an astonishing 5 times! This means, second, that those of us climbing along at $15,000 or $20,000 a year, getting our $1,000+ in tax breaks on our home mortgage and debt interest *remain powerless victims* of those whose discretionary income is available for such higher power pursuits as financing city, state, and national elections, or determining the direction of foundation grants and the price of oil. To compound the irony, we average people finance our own undermining by having to pay the bill for these special tax breaks.

If you make:	tax loopholes save you each year:
$ 5,000–10,000	$ 339
10,000–15,000	651
15,000–20,000	1,181
20,000–25,000	1,931
25,000–50,000	3,897
50,000–100,000	11,912
100,000–500,000	41,840
500,000–1,000,000	202,751
Over 1,000,000	720,490

We are not so much a middle-class society as a country of wage earners and wealth owners, with little mobility between. Nevertheless, we persist in calling ourselves middle, dream of moving up, and so vote our aspirations while being furious at those who freeload behind. We support the established system of deference by our own attitudes and actions.

Thus we ratify our own defeat—and *go into debt*. Becoming somebody in this middle-class race has become for too many of us something we purchase on account. Item: the relationship of family income to family debt shows a startling increase of 100 percent in average indebtedness over twenty years ago. And that figure does not include mortgage indebtedness. Increasingly, we seem to be developing a new kind of company store, with people locked into jobs by paychecks already locked into monthly credit payments.

"Still, we did it for the kids; so they could get a good education and get out of it all."

Passing On the Wounds of Status

Partly this hope works, but very partly. Seen in one way, a college education is one of the better bets going. A college graduate earns an average of $4,000 more per year over his lifetime than his high-school counterpart. But this does not move him from the wage-earner category into wealth-owner status. Moreover, there is another way to look at college. When you reckon that 60 percent of us now go on to some form of higher education, while less than 15 percent graduate with a four-year college degree, there is an awesome amount of failure—especially if you are a college teacher and must preside over it.

This failure rate is one of the ironic results of measuring people by the classroom bell curve. Still, perhaps it is not just ironic. In a society where the hierarchies of success are as steeply pyramided as ours, the sorting and filing system must begin its fundamental task at an early age. That task is to teach people how to fail without complaint and to take out their frustration against fellow failures—"B" running against "B" and "C" against "C" under the sovereign gaze of the person behind the desk who owns the system.

Moreover, there are sorting systems within sorting systems, even for the relatively successful. Take the fact that I teach at Temple University in Philadelphia, a large public university that services the general populace of the city. To speak with a cold and calculating eye, the function of Temple in the social ecology of Philadelphia is to produce, as it were, certified public accountants. It is to manufacture those who will loyally *work for,* and for less money than, those who graduated, let us say, from Yale. (The best of our students train to become doctors or lawyers or teachers, to get professional credentials as leverage against just being swallowed in this situation.)

Some people answer, "They had their chance; they took the Scholastic Aptitude Test and it answered back 'No Yale.' It's their own fault."

This answer is curiously similar to one received by a recent research team studying working-class parents. In *The Hidden Injuries of Class,* Richard Sennett and Jonathan Cobb[12] found that working-class persons often have two basic categories of self-interpretation by which they seek to make sense of their lives. One is self-accusation. They see themselves as failures and by their own fault. What else in a land of freedom of opportunity? "Look," said one of them, "it's nobody's fault but mine I got stuck where I did." The self completes

its social defeat by directing its anger against itself. The second idea
that grasped the workers was self-sacrifice. Many of these parents
made sense out of what was happening to them on the grounds of
sacrificing themselves for the kids. "We did it all for you" was a
refrain echoing through the standard rituals of family discourse.

The psychological impact of this elemental ambivalence—"I'm a
failure, but you should love and respect me because I did it all for
you"—passes the wounds of status on from one generation to the
next. The story told between parents and children in these and a good
many middle-class families cripples rather than vitalizes the next
generation. This is reflected in the relatively high incidence of
authoritarian ways of raising kids. If Sennett and Cobb are right,
many of the parents studied viewed themselves not as models to be
followed but as warnings, as lessons in failure.

Suspecting their own competence, they lacked fundamental and
automatic trust in their offspring. Their kids were not born winners,
but with careful watching and discipline they might be *made* into
winners. As one worker put it, "I haven't got it up here; but my kids
are smart; *I make 'em that way*." Sadly but inevitably, the children
pick up the hidden signal, the suspicion of mediocre endowment.
Usually they don't even get to college, much less through it. But even
if they do, there is an interesting process now well under way there,
too. And that is that their education will, among other things,
probably be an education in indebtedness.

For educational administrators caught in the squeeze between
tight financial resources and sky-rocketing institutional costs, the
programs of deferred payment and government-guaranteed student
loans come as a delightful escape. They can raise tuition with a clear
conscience, and, more to the point, without emptying their
classrooms. But it is far from an escape for the student.

He begins to pay back his debt after graduating. The interest rate
on these loans is such that he is likely to have to return a third again as
much as he actually paid. And what happens if he meets the girl of his
heart at school, and she, like him, has a debt? Well, that's quite a
financial merger.

Here is a young couple—having attained college educations in
order to increase their analytical perspective upon society and to
improve job *mobility* and freedom of life-style *choice*—starting their

marriage in debt to the tune of, shall we say, $6,000 (according to recent Health, Education and Welfare Department statistics, a conservative estimate). They need a car. They need furniture, appliances, and rent for the apartment, and they would like to save a little for a down payment on a house. So she goes to work, and they put off having children for a while. (How long, and with what effect?) Recent birth statistics, which have fallen off sharply for this particular group, indicate concern not so much for population growth as for minimal family solvency. The same may well be true for the emerging two child family ideal. That is an ideal that lets mother go back to work earlier.

Is this a passage into freedom by means of education? Locked into jobs a big chunk of whose paycheck is already taken each month in installment payments, our couple is taught not so much freedom as a premature subservience. Strapped by monthly strain, they easily become cowed by the given system of deference, with its precarious ladder leading upwards toward (someday) the light. After all, "Be quiet and stay in your place" is what education has traditionally taught us.

On the Run and Looking for Comfort

One of the earliest and most successful instruments of the American way of teaching was *The McGuffey Reader,* which taught generations of the hopeful and aspiring how to read and thus improve themselves. Here is a selection from one of its more illustrious admonitions.

> Once or twice though you should fail,
> Try, Try Again;
> If you would, at last, prevail,
> Try, Try Again;
> If we strive, 'tis no disgrace,
> Though we may not win the race;
> What should you do in that case?
> Try, Try Again.[13]

It is, you can see, instruction in the loneliness of the long-distance runner. Why "loneliness"?

Because to be a *middle*-class people is to be a people lost in space. It is to live forever "in-between," suffering from an infinite loneliness inside as we are reduced to endlessly measuring ourselves against an elusive outside standard. The middle is a class embarrassed about itself, never quite in possession of its pride. It runs from those behind—the failures, the nobodys, the ones who get pushed around and have to swallow it. And it strives after those ahead—where people feel full and self-confident. Middle is a tender and trembling place, full of hope and hurt.

The facts of this middle-class anxiety and search for escape are attested to in a recently compiled list of jobs which people feel are "most desirable." What is interesting is that the more prestigious jobs are not necessarily those that pay the most, but those which reflect the greatest *internal substance and accomplishment.* The chart shows the percentage desirability of various types of work according to a poll by the National Opinion Research Corporation in 1947 and again in 1963.[14]

Occupation	March, 1947 Rank [of Preference]	June, 1963 Rank [of Preference]
U.S. Supreme Court Justice	1	1
Physician	2.5	2
Scientist	8	3.5
College professor	8	8
Lawyer	18	11
Minister	13	17.5
Banker	10.5	24.5
Building contractor	34	31.5
Bookkeeper	51.5	49.5
Traveling salesman for wholesale concern	51.5	57
Singer in a nightclub	74.5	74

The chart demonstrates that the jobs most desired are those that refer to a life lived from the strength and fullness of one's insides— protected and comforted from the relentlessly measuring process. What is wanted is escape from the loneliness of the long-distance performer and the indeterminate way he gets stolen from himself by the assessing eyes of others.

This escape is what the Reverend Norman Vincent Peale is all about. Dr. Peale established his brilliant career upon the psychic anxieties to which the structural realities of a *middle*-class society give birth. His gospel is one of inner power. Already in his first big seller, *The Art of Living,* he established his central message: ". . . applied Christianity helps people to tap [the] reservoir of *power within* themselves." [15] There followed a whole series of revealing titles: *You Can Win, A Guide to Confident Living,* and of course the fabulously successful *The Power of Positive Thinking.* These books were filled with homilies about how to fill and make potent one's inner space—"How to Get Rid of Your Inferiority Complex," "How to Think Your Way to Success," "How to Achieve a Calm Center for Your Life." [16]

The lexicon of Dr. Peale's writings provides a mind-boggling commentary upon the psychic traumas that haunt the middle class. But no one seemed embarrassed by it all—embarrassed and saddened, that is, because of what it says about the people who need and buy these nostrums. In fact, rather than getting sued for slander, Dr. Peale was elevated to the post of top healer and comforter of those who know themselves as perpetually in-between. However, Peale healed his flock not by removing them from the condition of their disease but by leaving them in the *middle,* refueled road-runners forever looking to be filled—and forever suffering new emptiness. This group, once secularized, likes "depth" psychology because it corresponds to their fundamental social condition.

Housewives, mothers, workers, and average suburban Americans—haunted as we are by a misplaced deference—where do we go if we want comfort in fact rather than in fiction? Where do we go when we begin to sense the frozen realities behind our wide-open dreams?

This question was posed in a letter from a young man in response to an article of mine on the plight of the middle class. He said in part:

I read your article . . . and am in full agreement with it. I feel that the most important point you make concerns the well-being of the family unit. As a secondary school teacher I can tell you that the great majority of discipline problems are found in families having both parents working. I have discovered cases where both parents hold more than one job. . . . I myself am faced with this problem. In buying a single family home in New Jersey, I have burdened the family budget to such an extent that I will need two part-time jobs to stave off actual poverty. The question then is, what is to be done? Political action is useless. The Republicans are preoccupied with aiding big business and the Democrats with the lower class. . . . What is your answer?

Now, there's the problem, there in those last two lines. With one party for the rich and the other, so the young man thinks, for the lower class (in fact, both parties serve the rich), there's no place politically for middle-class people like himself to go. And there are millions like him, groping their way through the myth of the middle, wondering why nobody's their friend.

What can be done? We can start by disabusing ourselves of misplaced titles. We are not so much "middle" as we are *wage earners* in a system of deference set up to service *wealth owners*. Our natural allies—the 75 percent of us making less than $17,000 a year—are those running the stampede alongside and behind us. To exhaust ourselves by each pushing his own way forward is to fuel the general price rise, and so end up running frantically just to stay in the same place. What we need instead is a redistribution of burdens. For we have, indeed, a welfare state. But the people benefiting most by the public dole are the wealthy few at the top who each year receive $77 billion in special tax breaks while the rest of us do the rugged individualism thing, even at $20,000 and $25,000. For in terms of statistical averages, only those with an income above $35,000 can begin to get their income shifted over into the tax-sheltered property and interest category.

True, these old contradictions in our social system have been around a long time without generating an effective revolt on the part of the exploited majority. But certain new contradictions, now emerging, may add the critical difference to set the avalanche going.

Old Myths and New Contradictions

Paul Samuelson, Nobel laureate in economics, has pointed out: "If we made an income pyramid out of a child's blocks, with each layer portraying $1,000 of income, the peak would be far higher than the Eiffel Tower, but almost all of us would be within a yard of the ground." [17] What is perhaps even more remarkable than the fact of this concentration of income and wealth is its relative continuity over time since the founding of our country. We have been living with this kind of skewed economic picture, and evidently have been willing to since our beginning—in Philadelphia in 1774, 10 percent of the population owned 89 percent of the taxable property in that city.

This continuity of concentrated wealth is especially remarkable when we reckon the immense population growth over the past one hundred years and the seemingly successful integration of these millions of poor immigrants into our society. What made this possible was the fortunate coincidence of this massive in-migration with the rise of industrialization. Industrialization made it possible to expand rapidly overall economic activity and so produce goods and services at a rapid enough pace that the middle 70 percent of us could improve our life-style without significantly disturbing the top 10 percent who monopolized better than 50 percent of the wealth. Of course, this rapid expansion of the economic pie also increased just as rapidly the amount of discretionary income available at the top and thus, in power terms, increased the top's ability to control.

What we have had then is not so much upward mobility as an expanding economy which gave the illusion to the many of moving up while in fact solidifying the hold of the few on top.

Because the many believed the myth of the middle, they continued to run on. The middle illusion provided them with hope. The myth defused the anger that would go with a surer grasp on the actual system of advantages. It provided a feeling, wholly inaccurate, of common brotherhood in a world of relative equals—"Why, even the boss thinks of himself as middle class." And for those on top, the middle myth sanctioned their inordinate income and advantage on the basis of its ready availability if not to everyone, at least to the worthy—"After all, President Lincoln was born in a log cabin."

Richard Parker in his book, *The Myth of the Middle Class,* has accurately named the realities of America hiding behind our myths. "America," Parker says, "has created a stable moneyed aristocracy, admitting few newcomers but capable of surviving the upturns and downturns of all political and economic climates."[18] I would only want to add—"up until now." For the thing that made this whole game possible—the rapid expansion of the economy that provided for the many the illusion of moving up in the world—is coming into a new set of contradictions which I believe will bring all this to a shattering halt.

If I am right, then we are on the edge of either a majoritarian-based fundamental restructuring of our society or an open repression of the many by and for the sake of the few. In the latter case, what would be new about the situation is not the exploitation, but the fact that it would be out in the open and forcefully imposed.

The new contradictions I am speaking of have to do with the onset of the steeply rising costs of energy and raw materials in all advanced industrial nations, as well as the steadily expanding cost to industry for cleaning up its own pollution. The rapid expansion of our country's economy depended upon a kind of wide-open world, where cheap fuels and raw materials, docile heads of underdeveloped states, and endless supplies of fresh air and water could be taken for granted. They no longer can be.

The result is that into the foreseeable future it will cost us a good deal more just to stay at the same economic level. Where will this money come from in an economy where the Gross National Product will have to slow down in its mad dash? From the middle? That will end its dream. And the resulting anger will focus on those ahead rather than behind. The rising costs of the new economic world realities will force either a redistribution of the burdens in our society or a barricading of themselves by the highly advantaged few.

2 TRYING

"My brother is not my keeper. But when he
can, he keeps me down."
—Neill Rathgelo, Temple University

Inflation has proved a successful way of disguising what is happening in America—or more exactly, what is not happening. At least, until recently the rate of inflation was slow enough so that people did not realize its full effect. As long as inflation remains unnoticed, people can think things are getting better, when they may be staying just about the same in terms of actual purchasing power. What does this persistent rise in the cost of living do to the average person's hopes?

The Price of Living Respectably

We are, we are told, an affluent country. Which means that
—even if we are not a middle-class nation but a society of a few wealth owners and many wage earners, and
—even if the majority have to pick up the price tag for the privileges of the advantaged few,
still we have a comfortable way of life, and so we should be grateful.

Unfortunately, this proposed consolation is neither adequate repayment for our unequal treatment nor accurate in terms of our private life-styles. Most of us are not affluent but overworked and running hard just to stay in place. We can see this when we analyze carefully the average family budget. Before I started to research the statistics, I consistently overestimated the actual figures by something like $5,000 a year. Popular rhetoric and commercial advertising had given me such an overly optimistic view. What the statistics made me do was imagine my way into the truth that even in 1971, according to the U.S. Bureau of Labor statistics, it took a family of four $10,971 to sustain a "moderate family budget."[1] Remembering the fact that *fewer than half* of our country's households attained that level that year, let us see how this nearly $11,000 (or $9,186 after taxes and Social Security deductions) breaks down in terms of itemized household costs.[2]

> *Food*—$50 a week, including every restaurant lunch and football hotdog.
> *Housing*—$219 a month for all housing expenses, such as mortgage, utilities, furniture, new screens, and even window cleaner.
> *Transportation*—$964 yearly, or $4 per work day, including paying for and insuring the car, and repairing, fueling, and parking it. (The Bureau also estimated the car would need to last seven to eight years.)
> *Medical*—$612, including health insurance, prescriptions, doctor's office visits, and so on. (If a child needs braces for his teeth, it would mean sacrificing from another category.)
> *Clothing and personal care*—$1,196 yearly. (Of this, Mrs. Middle's share would be about $275 for everything from lingerie to lipstick.)
> $563 yearly—to cover union dues, life insurance, Christmas presents, and charities.
> $684 yearly—to cover entertainment, radio, records, newspapers, TV, vacations, toys, movie and other tickets, and education.

Notice some of the things which this budget makes clear about a moderate family life-style. First, there is very little discretionary income—nothing, for example, set aside for savings. Every penny the family earns must be tightly budgeted just to keep even with the bills. Unforeseen dental or expensive medical costs not covered by insurance, an unexpected car bill or suddenly necessary plumbing repair—any of these presses a family living on such a budget either into borrowing or into looking for new sources of income.

Moreover, notice how impacted those last two lines in the family budget are. Charities must compete with union dues, life insurance, and Christmas presents for a place in the average family budget. What does this do to the financial base of such voluntary organizations as churches and synagogues, or YM and YWCAs which depend fundamentally upon the charitable giving of middle Americans? Especially in a period of steep inflation, the sources of independent financing in our society dry up, with a consequent economic undermining of institutions not securely funded by government or by the upper class.

Another illustration of the tight financial situation of average families is education, which must compete against TV and records,, entertainment and vacations. With the soaring costs of college, is it any wonder that Mr. and Mrs. Middle can no longer afford to pay for their children's education without (1) having the wife go back to work, (2) getting heavily into borrowing, or (3) putting the kids into debt with educational loans? Put simply, the middle class is getting edged out of anything except the least expensive state college education. And the same kind of thing may be true in housing. With the price of buying a house rising at 9 percent yearly, a U.S. House Banking subcommittee heard expert testimony that "Over 60 percent of the families in the country today can't afford to buy a home."[3]

A more detailed analysis of what the government calls "the moderate family budget" reveals that for any kind of significant life-style improvement—such as getting a new car, buying a new house, sending the children to college, and so on—this family must turn to new sources of income or buy their status on credit. Is this a picture of comfortable affluence, of financial security beyond month-to-month anxiety? I think not. This conclusion becomes even more clear when you factor in the recent steep rise in inflation.

According to the same U.S. Bureau of Labor, the "moderate family budget" we have been looking at would have had to be a full $1,000 more in 1972 than in 1971 just to stay even. And in 1973, the family would have needed another $1,200 raise to keep from falling behind. That represents a 10 percent wage increase each of those years. In fact, the average working man got only half of that increase. In urban areas the situation was worse. In New York City, for example, it was estimated that, for a moderate standard of living, a family of four would need an annual income of $13,453, which was up by 13.2 percent over the previous year.[4]

In a word, middle Americans have been persistently *downwardly mobile* in the years since 1971, with few prospects of doing much better than leveling out the descending curve of their life-style over the years immediately ahead. This reality has proved especially disturbing to *the sense of fairness* that lies necessarily at the foundation of our democratic allegiance. Why? While the majority have had to cut back in their pecuniary expectations, those who set the emulative standards at the top of our society have continued to increase their spending ability. The resulting inability to meet rising expectations begins to attack directly the average man's way of making sense out of his working years, on the traditional grounds of "getting a fair deal" and "moving up a little each year." Average Americans are today being forced to reconsider just what is actually being done to them by the managers of our society who claim to be their friends.

They are finding, if they study the statistics, that while the poor and middle class increased (slightly) their share of the national wealth from 1950 to 1968, in the four years that followed (1969–1973), the trend was reversed. The highest and second-highest fifths of the population each increased their share of wealth while the middle and lower fifths declined.

As the lower income groups in our society vie with each other over a decreasing share of the national wealth while battling to survive inflation, our basic social contract is threatened. Our democratic society is based upon a sense of fairness for all, and its stability is severely strained by a broad sense of unfair treatment.[5] When we look at the meagerness of even a "moderate family budget" in 1971 (realizing that $1,000 more was needed in 1972, and even another $1,200 to stay even in 1973, and so on each year), we are led to ask whether the meaning of America as the promise of freedom of opportunity has kept faith with the average people. Or is this opportunity and chance at the good life reserved for the special few at the top? A more accurate picture of America begins to emerge: namely, a table of enormous affluence at which a very few people sit while the rest of us fight with each other over the crumbs that fall from the table, permanently barred from pulling up our own chairs.

Why Inflation?

Since the steep rise in inflation has in the past several years brought into sharp focus the realities (they have been there hidden, for a long time before that) which today assault the family dreams of average Americans, we should take a closer look at its causes.

In his highly informative book, *The New Inflation,* economist G. L. Bach reminds us that inflation has been *a persistent phenomenon in our country for thirty years now.* "We live," he points out, "in an *age* of inflation. Since World War II prices in the United States have more than doubled."[6] Looked at more closely, in the period from 1959–1969 the consumer price index jumped 35 percent. Add on the rise in federal, state, and local taxes and one gets a total figure of a 41 percent increase in just ten years.

THE AVERAGE WAGE EARNER HAS NOT KEPT UP; IN FACT HE'S LOST GROUND. The purchasing power of the average weekly paycheck measured in 1957–1959 dollars peaked in 1965 at a high of $88.06, and by 1970 it was down to $85.35.[7] As we are fully aware, inflationary costs since that time have only worsened.

One source of this persistent rise in the cost of living is *taxation.* State and local taxes have grown from 7 percent of the Gross National Product to 12 percent in less than twenty years.[8] Paralleling these taxes has been the imposition of new excise taxes and a steadily rising base rate for the Social Security tax. In 1970 a wage earner paid Social Security on only the first $9,000 of income. By 1974 this base rate had been raised to $13,200 for an overall tax increase, albeit hidden, of some $300 per year. By 1975 the base was raised again to over $14,000.

Note that this Social Security tax rise has been targeted rather precisely upon Mr. and Mrs. Middle, since the base rate has been going up each year almost exactly equal with the rise in average family income. Indeed, it is generally true that the kinds of taxes which are growing are the very ones which impact most heavily upon poor- and average-income households. Using Social Security taxes again as an example, they rose at a rate of 41 percent over the six-year period from 1962 to 1968 relative to the median income at that time of

$6,000–$8,000. But if you were in the $25,000+ bracket, the tax rise represented only a 22 percent increase in relation to income.[9] Beware: speculation on extending socially subsidized health care has tended to look to Social Security—i.e., regressive—tax funding rather than new resources generated through tax reform.

This reversal of the intention built into the idea of a progressive tax (pegged in terms of ability to pay) can be strikingly shown by charting the way in which the rising state and local taxes (income, property, and sales) have affected various family budgets.[10]

Income Bracket	State and Local Taxes as Percent of Income
under $2,000	11.3
2,000–3,999	9.4
4,000–5,999	8.5
6,000–7,999	7.7
8,000–9,999	7.2
10,000–14,999	6.5
15,000 and over	5.9

Comparatively, the poor pay most, and Mr. Middle is next.

In sum, there has been a *hidden taxation inflation* over the past two decades, the results of which have been *most damaging precisely on modest and average family budgets*. To compound the irony, just trying to stay even with the rising cost of living forces families into ever higher *income* (and tax) brackets as well, without delivering any additional purchasing power. Meanwhile, Congress has rewarded corporations with a *tax cut*. Today, only about one-seventh of the total federal tax revenue comes from businesses, whereas in 1960 corporate taxes accounted for nearly one-fourth of the federal revenues.[11]

Besides taxation, there has been a loss in corporate efficiency, a loss whose price tag has been passed on to the consumer. Business is having an ever larger part of its tax bill paid for by average Americans while, in return, it is producing less efficiently and therefore at higher costs. At least this seems to be the implication of a recent Federal Trade Commission's *Economic Report on Corporate Mergers*. The larger the corporation the bigger break it gets in terms of the Investment Tax Credit. But does increased size lead to a higher level of efficiency, and so overall lower costs for the public? The Federal

Trade Commission's report thought not. "The recent and past experience of large, rapidly merging firms," it said, "appears to warrant genuine skepticism as to the potential for management to capably operate large, far-flung diversified enterprises."[12] A study by the staff of the Cabinet Committee on Price Stability concluded: "This [merger] movement appears to be propelled by special financial and speculative consideration rather than by the pursuit of efficiency through large-scale business organizations."[13]

After Watergate, I should think that we will want to ask much more carefully just how our tax policies—and the business interests and election finances of those who write our tax laws—affect the inflation rate the rest of us are forced to pay. Here is another illustration of the degree to which the well-being of Mr. and Mrs. Middle is *not* what America is presently all about.

However, to analyze the inflation caused by tax and profit increases, and the passed-on costs of business inefficiency, is not yet to reach the heart, the driving power, that sustains the persistent inflation push in our society. Rather, we must see how centrally inflation is bound up with the fundamental logic of our country's system of public meanings.

Thorstein Veblen, in his classic *The Theory of the Leisure Class,* has shown the degree to which America was never so much the open society as the *wide*-open society, not so much the land of equal opportunity as the land of opportunity to establish oneself in unequal advantage and ostentation over one's neighbor. Veblen showed the degree to which we are fueled as a people by the fevers of "pecuniary emulation" and an insatiable, restless straining for "invidious distinction."[14]

How can we receive as many hours of instruction through TV and magazine advertising as we have and still remain so largely unconscious of the actual style of our culture? Take, for example, the kitchens displayed in popular magazine soap advertisements. Watch what appears in the background of these ads—the kitchen appliances, the look of newness, the lawn and trees outside the window which define the taken-for-granted standard package of pecuniary emulation. By doing a brief historical comparison, one can follow the evolution of this standard package over the years, as first an electric stove, then a refrigerator, then a clothes washer and dryer, and finally a dishwasher, garbage disposal, and even trash compactor are added as part of the taken-for-granted backdrop for the soap ad.

This development documents the evolution of the dimensions of our emulative imagination—that is, the standard judgments of comparison we bring upon ourselves in terms of providing an adequate public "face," the display of our moving up and becoming affluent. Such an historical unfolding is instructive because it gives concrete evidence of the way in which this taken-for-granted package of middle-class self-respect remains essentially open-ended and insatiable. Veblen saw the underlying logic here. He pointed out:

> In order to stand well in the eyes of the community, it is necessary to come up to a certain, somewhat indefinite, conventional standard of wealth. . . . But as fast as a person makes new acquisitions, and becomes accustomed to the resulting new standard of wealth, the new standard forthwith ceases to afford appreciably greater satisfaction than the earlier standard did.[15]

Here is the internal psychic engine of what we referred to earlier as the middle-class endless road-running. It is, to use Veblen's term, "a race for reputability." Its essential endlessness was shown by Veblen when he pointed out that people in each level of society look to the next highest level life-style as their ideal and strive to live up to that ideal.[16] Which is to say that the commodities that constitute an acceptable public display are constantly passing out of date, not simply because of style change or built-in deterioration (e.g., light bulbs, dishwashers, cars, and so on), but because of emulative obsolescence. They no longer confirm our standing, our pecuniary accomplishment.

Put this factor together with the way in which the tax laws are skewed to the advantage of those ahead, and you come upon a devastating irony: we average people in our society financially underwrite our own persistent weariness and endless running after self-respect. Somehow the people ahead always just get more ahead.

We can feel, I suppose, superior to all this and derisively label it "materialism." Yet we should recall that in a society that thinks of itself as "middle class" and "upwardly mobile" and so already enjoying "affluence," the pressure to make sense of one's life this way comes down with the whole weight of the surrounding cultural reinforcements. Where we are most naked and needful as individuals is always at this level of the continuous supply of persuasive public meanings. Otherwise we do not know where we are or how to act or what we should want. Understanding this situation does not remove the tragedy, but it does remove some of the bitter, too easy superiority of observing a man, like Richard Nixon, *who climbed all his life.* Thus as vice-president, he was never even invited into the private quarters of the White House; but as president, he married his daughter to Ike's only grandson—a winner at last—for a while.

The sense of forlornness which surrounds our standard American identity, this man-in-the-middle who is forever on the run, was given eloquent voice by the playwright Arthur Miller in his *Death of a Salesman.* Standing over the grave of Willy Loman, his only friend Charley explains:

> You don't understand: Willy was a salesman. And for a salesman, there is no rock bottom to the life. He don't put a bolt to a nut, he don't tell you the law or give you medicine. He's a man way out there in the blue, riding on a smile and a shoeshine. And when they start not smiling back—that's an earthquake. And then you get yourself a couple of spots on your hat, and you're finished. Nobody dast blame this man. A salesman is got to dream, boy. It comes with the territory.[17]

We shall return to this analysis of the psychic makeup of middle-class people numerous times in the chapters to come. But it is important to examine the theme here in order to see how it builds inflation into the very psychic roots of our society. Why? Economist G. L. Bach points out:

> . . . the money illusion has deceived some income recipients into thinking their real incomes have risen more than they actually have. It is important to remember that, in such a world, inflation can end only when some groups give up part of their real income claims, knowingly or unknowingly.[18]

Precisely! Inflation has deeply to do with the disproportions of wealth in our society, as this interacts with the psychology of a middle-class people.

We can outline this point in the following way:

1. People in the middle measure their social status by comparing themselves with the consumer accomplishments of their "superiors."

2. Meanwhile, all this pushing and shoving in the middle does not affect the wealthy few, who maintain their size wealth at a

percentage rate of increase equal to the middle class—i.e., their *relative relationship* does not change.

3. Moreover, because there are fewer persons at the top to share this increase, the economic distance between the advantaged few and the many in the middle continues to grow.

4. This causes a crisis of comparative self-respect among average Americans. They work more jobs and go into debt in order somehow to make it, while having to watch those who really are making it move out ever further in front of them, setting ever higher standards for emulation.

5. *Conclusion:* The present unequal tax system (income, estate, and corporate) is a major cause of long-range inflation, because it sustains the purchasing power of those who set the patterns of consumption at the same time as it reduces the ability of those in the middle ever to fulfill those patterns. Thus, consumer demand is constantly inflated beyond productivity.

The inevitable conclusion is that if we are to manage effectively the problem of inflation, we can do this only through revising the size of the wealth shares that go to various groups in our society. Otherwise, we are only painting over the problem. As Professor Bach points out, "If we want to preserve the value of our monetary unit, then we must reconcile conflicting income interests through a voluntary working consensus—not by hoping to fool most of the people most of the time."[19] Bach, who has served as senior economist to the Federal Reserve Board, suggests that between 20 and 40 percent of the present tax-sheltered income shares from profits and interests might be shifted over into income going to wage and salary earners, without undermining the central forces necessary to fuel our economy. This change would involve sharply curtailing tax loopholes for large personal and corporate wealth, and lowering taxes on the poor- and middle-income brackets.

Unfortunately, recent administrations—whether controlled by Republicans or Democrats—have not shown any real willingness to take hold of inflation at this fundamental level. They have depended, instead, upon lulling the people to sleep with wage increments wrapped inside of an unnoticed long-range inflation, which leaves average Americans vaguely wondering why it is not better for them after all these years of moving up. For as Bach clearly states: "The gains from continually rising prices as a social lubricant and mollifier of class conflict are largely illusory."[20]

Sooner or later, this nettle of inflation, based on our wealth structure, must be grasped. And the interesting thing about the steep inflation rate we have recently been experiencing is that it sets loose a majority discomfort and sense of betrayal which could be mobilized for this task. The obvious problem is that so many of our national political leaders are themselves wealthy persons, or beholden to wealthy interests, who stand only to lose from a more equal distribution of our national wealth. Insofar as our elected representatives refuse to act on this basic issue, they should at least *stop claiming* to be our friends or to represent our interests.

The obvious and clear need of average Americans is for an *economically more equal America.* Under these circumstances alone can the emulative fires be banked, the stampede of the middle class be abated, and so some sense brought into our senseless running. Until this happens, the American Dream will continue washing out into the wastelands of inflation, and we will have a forlorn sense that the "good life" somehow constantly keeps slipping out of our grasp.

Without a fundamental restructuring of our wealth distribution, the natural response to long-term inflation is to work longer hours or more jobs, or keep up face by extending our emulative capacities through consumer credit, all strategies of desperation.

Overworked and Worried

"In April of 1970, Assistant Secretary of Labor Jerome Rosow placed on President Nixon's desk a memorandum entitled 'The Problems of the Blue-Collar Worker.'"[21] The report concluded that

> when general wage rate increases are added to increased individual earnings due to promotion, real income has somewhat less than doubled in the past two decades, which is still not enough to cover the cost of the *same* standard of living throughout the period.[22]

But how, then, do these families keep up with the American Dream? How do they make sense out of their public lives in a society of upward mobility and middle-class affluence? In his highly praised book on *Blue-Collar Life,* Arthur Shostak names the realities here. "Budget inflation, inadequacy, and disparity demonstrate the serious erosion that has occurred in the worker's economic position."

Shostak concludes: "For all the talk of joining the 'great central mass,' most workers have actually failed to share in the semiaffluence of the postwar years; many in 1967 could not even manage a stringent 'moderate' living budget."[23]

It is a mistake to think this is true only for blue-collar workers. Most white-collar and service workers have felt the same bewilderment at working harder but seeming to get further behind all the time. Only those in the higher income brackets managed to move out in front of inflation and improve their life-style a little. The rest, so the figures show, began to look for alternate sources of income to supplement their strained family budgets.

In 1967 the largest income group—25.1 percent of the total *white* population—received between $7,000 and $9,999. But to make it into this income level, 56.1 percent of these families had to have two or more wages. At the $10,000 to $12,000 level the families needing more than one wage to attain this income rose to 66.9 percent; and at the $12,000 to $15,000 mark the percent was an incredible 75.3 percent.[24] Only in those families making more than $20,000 yearly *in 1967* did second-wage dependency drop off sharply. What we have is not so much middle-class affluence as middle-class moonlighting and exhaustion.

And none of these figures documents the traffic patterns and turmoil of black families trying to make it! But an ominous statistic gives us a clue. In the past twenty years the suicide rate among black males has risen 33 percent, as compared with a 10 percent rise for whites. Spotlighting a horrifying contradiction, black psychologist Napoleon Vaughn of Philadelphia has concluded that "it's the concept of equal opportunity that has contributed mostly to black suicide."[25]

Many of the second wage figures we have been looking at came not from moonlighting husbands but from working wives. In the spring of 1974, Herbert Stein, chairman of the president's Board of Economic Advisors, was blaming inflation on "the people." While doing so, he let slip an interesting statistic. The average family, he pointed out, now has 1.7 *workers* in it. Said more precisely, over half of the families making $12,500 (the 1973 median income) did so only because *both husband and wife worked.* These are the family budget realities that lie behind the overall figures which show a 22 percent increase in male workers from 1940 to 1970, but a 131 percent increase in female workers during the same period.

Holding down a job may be liberating for some women. However, for a sharply increased number of wives it is not freedom but economic necessity that is behind it all. This truth comes home with special clarity when we reflect that the kinds of jobs available to most women are low-paying and menial, involved with what is often demeaning and obsequious game playing with male bosses. Moreover, most of these women continue to be held almost exclusively responsible for the housework duties at home.

Moonlighting, working wives, exhaustion, and persistent worry and fighting over money—this is the picture of reality which peeks out from behind many of those middle-class dreams. And usually we cannot even talk about it with each other. To do so would mean admitting to such an "un-American" feeling as a sense of economic inadequacy. The myths of upward mobility, affluence, and self-help create great silences among those who suffer from middle-class budgetary worries. The protest gets deflected from society into fights with the children, alcoholism, divorce, and early heart attack. Thus, we are not brought together by our public myths of meaning, but we are kept apart. We shy away from sharing our money worries lest such sharing demean our public standing. We learn to bear what we think are our private embarrassments in the midst of what is in fact a *public* disgrace—the structure of concentrated wealth. We do not comfort each other where we hurt because where we hurt is where we have been taught to *measure each other*. We impoverish friendship and feed the system of inequality by our lonely and unspoken frustrations.

Besides moonlighting and working wives, the expansion of consumer credit has been another way of keeping the dream going. It is a way of maintaining middle-class face, at least for a while, when middle-class truths cannot be bared.

The underlying structural reality is that the "wealth" which most of us own is not *wealth-producing wealth,* but income-consuming items, such as cars and houses and appliances. Economic surveys tend to record all of this simply as "wealth" and so fail to register the degree to which the figures represent also a kind of indebtedness not only in regard to the cost of operation, but also in the style of purchase.

Americans owed in 1973 a record $821.3 billion in debts which range from charge accounts to mortgages. That is triple the figure of only fourteen years ago. Moreover, it represents an increase of 27 percent since late 1971 as compared with only an 18 percent rise in after-tax income in the same period. All of this says that people are not only more deeply in debt, but also they are further in debt *in relationship to their overall family income*—and so, ever deeper into end-of-the-month panic.

After years of looking benignly upon this rise of consumer credit, the American business establishment is beginning to show signs of sudden worry. The *Wall Street Journal* of December 11, 1973, ran a front-page article on the possibility of a potentially disastrous credit overexpansion. Quoting from the Census Bureau economist John Gorman, the article reported that a record 23 percent portion of after-tax income is now being taken up on interest charges and repayments on mortgages and installment loans. The article noted with concern that economist Leonard Lempert says that the rise of credit use since 1970 dwarfs anything on the record books, showing mortgage debt soaring at annual rates above $50 billion and consumer installment credit leaping by more than $20 billion a year.[26]

Now when anticipated income increases get eaten up by rapid inflation, a real credit crisis begins to appear. Families make their credit estimates on the basis of anticipated discretionary income— income after household musts have been taken care of. But inflation wipes out this anticipated little extra. As economist Gorman put it, borrowing may have been done by "people who didn't expect economic trouble" in the years ahead.[27]

The result is that the Mortgage Bankers Association is now reporting the highest number of mortgage delinquencies in twenty years. Consumer-loan delinquencies also reached a record high by February, 1974. And the kind of people in trouble has changed. John A. Kennedy, vice-president of the installment division of Provident National Bank in Philadelphia, points out:

> These are people that have lived under budgets that have allowed for borrowing, and they just can't make it anymore. These are good people, middle-class people, but they just can't keep up.[28]

We buy our middle-class face on credit—and end up losing face as we juggle bills and try to explain to creditors. Once again, we are *privately* embarrassed by our inability to live up to expectations.

The American middle class is more overworked and worried than it is affluent. The average family budget, even in relatively good times like 1971, has very little in it in the way of luxuries—viz., $50 per week to feed a family of four, $219 a month to house them, and so on. And when the 20-year routine inflation heats up and takes off, then that family begins to see clearly what has been going on all along: namely, that it is not moving up, that it enjoys little in the way of the Good Life—except in its dreams of the winning lottery ticket or TV quiz show.

But more than that, now the average middle-class family has even to begin figuring out how to cut back on the modest degree of decency it has managed to attain. It must administer its own *downward mobility.*

The New Austerity

"In November 1973, the Department of Agriculture reported: 'The sharpest drop in per capita food consumption in 15 years has occurred this year.'"[29] People were turning to cheaper foods or eating less, or both, with the result that real outlays (adjusted for price increases) dropped 5.4 percent below what they had been a year earlier. In the January-March quarter of 1974 the situation grew even worse with the rate of decline at 6.5 percent of the 1972 level. Looking at individual food items, we can see where Mr. and Mrs. Middle were tightening their belts. "'Red meat' consumption fell 7.1 percent . . . a decline described [by the Agricultural Department] as 'the most precipitous since 1948.' Egg consumption also fell sharply . . . 'bringing consumption to the lowest levels since the 1930s.'"[30]

Even while average Americans were eating less well, they still had to pay a higher proportion of their family income for food. In January, 1973, the "moderate" budget projected by the government showed food costing 36 percent of the take-home pay of a worker with three dependents. One year later, the figure had jumped to 42 percent—*almost half* the weekly income![31] Besides cutting back in the amount and quality of food, average Americans began spending less on "hard goods," such as automobiles, furniture, household equipment, and appliances. With the prices of nondurables like food, gasoline, and heating oil soaring, the middle class trimmed its expenses where it could. Expenditures for movies, vacations, and house repair all showed declines.

In short, the 1970s saw average Americans working more, eating less, going further into debt, worrying more about money, and generally enjoying life less. The good times had wandered off somewhere else, leaving the middle class puzzled and somehow feeling trapped.

And this new austerity is *not* likely to pass away quickly. It is rooted in the rapid rise in demand for goods and services in all advanced industrial nations and in the new demand from nonindustrial, supplier nations that their raw materials return to them a bigger piece of the economic action. That price is not being paid for out of corporate profits—as is shown by what Senator Henry Jackson called "the obscene profit-level of oil companies"—it is being passed on to the consumer.

Thus, while Mr. and Mrs. Middle are tightening their belts, postponing their dreams, and wondering for how long, corporate profits and corporate executive salaries have been soaring. According to a *New York Times'* financial report, average corporate profits before taxes were up 24 percent in 1973, a rate equaled only twice in the last twenty years, while the corporate tax rate this year will probably "slip to the lowest in at least two decades."[32] American living standards have been pulling apart down the center—the middle moving down while the top spenders continue to fatten their display of successful living at the top. As Stanford University economist John Gurley has said, "The fact is that the rich are not being soaked; instead, they are soaking up wealth very rapidly in ever-increasing amounts."[33]

The middle class experiences America not so much as a system of upward mobility as a kind of ongoing disappointment, where all the special breaks go to the few at the top. America seems somehow a system of unexpected failure, where a person works hard all his life and still does not get very far. Which is to say that the middle class, with its dreams and trying to realize its hopes, finds itself in a traffic jam of the struggling many, up against a roadblock called the privileged few.

3 PRIVILEGE

> "Communities divide themselves into the few and the many. The first are the rich and well-born, the other the mass of the people . . . turbulent and changing, they seldom judge or determine right. Give therefore to the first class a distinct, permanent share in Government."[1]
>
> —Alexander Hamilton

Most of us have believed that America enjoys the fruits of democratic government. In a nation which had to absorb millions of poor immigrants, this notion that every person has a fair chance is crucial for domestic tranquillity. The purpose of this chapter is to show that the opposite is largely the case. Hamilton's company of "the rich and the well-born" has effectively come into control of both economic and political power. This aristocracy of rule is disguised by the rhetoric of free elections (which in fact are very expensive) and the idea of freedom of opportunity (for those who finish college—preferably Harvard, Yale, or Princeton). In short, our society has a facade which is Jeffersonian democracy, behind which is the reality of Hamilton.

To establish my case, I will begin with the way wealth *is and remains* highly concentrated in our society by means of the successful manipulation of tax and estate laws. Then I will show how this wealth becomes politically powerful, using government to impose the interests of the few upon the many. Finally, I will demonstrate how a sizable portion of the social science establishment helps legitimate this situation by transforming the traditional notion of democracy—

rule by and for the people—into an apology for rule by an elite. Thus, while social scientists continue to talk about democracy, many of them no longer mean by it what the rest of us do.

Wealth Concentration

Six million families who made less than $3,000 a year in 1971 got $92 million in welfare payments. That same year, three thousand families each *making over $1 million* got "welfare" benefits of $2 billion 200 million. They benefited from a generous government tax subsidy. Hard to believe? Statistics show that the tax burden of the richest 1 percent of Americans *declined* from 33 to 26 percent in the last twenty-five years. In that same period, payroll taxes *quadrupled,* and property, sales, and excise taxes *doubled!* The burdens of paying for America have shifted significantly, to the distinct disadvantage of most of us.[2]

We find a concrete example of this tax welfare for the wealthy in the case of the late Ailsa Mellon Bruce, heir to the famous Andrew Mellon of Pittsburgh and the Mellon Bank/Westinghouse/Gulf Oil fortune. Mrs. Bruce died in 1969 leaving an estate "valued at $570,748,725—well over half a *billion* dollars." The tax on that size fortune should have been 77 percent, according to established rates. This steep inheritance tax was designed to respond effectively to America's claim to be a society of relatively equal opportunity, rather than frozen family wealth. Actually, the Bruce estate ended up paying $6½ million in death taxes, or a little over 1 percent.[3]

Mrs. Bruce's lawyers did better for her than average; although on an average, big estates do well enough. This is shown in the following chart. It demonstrates the successful fictionalization of the social intent implied by the seemingly steep inheritance tax.[4]

Gross Estate Size	Tax Rate Schedule	Actual Tax
$ 1—$2,000,000	33%—38%	21.0%
$ 2—$3,000,000	38%—42%	23.5%
$ 3—$5,000,000	42%—49%	25.6%
$ 5—$10,000,000	49%—61%	25.7%
$10—$20,000,000	61%—69% ⎫	
$20,000,000 and over	69+% ⎬	26.8%

The result of this tax escape is that some $10 billion is lost to the federal treasury each year. It is not an escape the rest of us enjoy. We have to pick up the added tax bill. As author Philip Stern has put it, "one man's loophole is another man's cross."[5] How does this public treasury raid take place?

As long as a person holds the stock he buys until he dies, he will never, under present law, have to pay income tax on it. This is true even though the stock may appreciate in value several times from $50,000, let us say, to $250,000. If upon his death his wife (or whoever) sells the stock quickly, there will be no "capital gains" tax assessed against the appreciated value (in our example, $200,000), since the Internal Revenue Service views the price of the stock as that at the time of death.

Moreover, a wealthy husband and wife can give away up to $6,000 a year to their children and grandchildren (or anyone else) and take a charitable deduction for it. The result is that an affluent couple with three children and their spouses and nine grandchildren could give away $90,000 tax free each year just to the immediate family. Similarly, a "marital deduction" of one-half the worth of the entire estate is available when it is left to a surviving wife. The adoption of this provision in 1948 lowered the estate tax revenues by about one-third. You and I have picked up the difference.

Or again, let us say that a person built a palatial home and gardens forty years ago for $2 million, which is assessed today at a value of $20 million. If he gives the house and grounds to a university, for example, to establish a conference site, the IRS lets that person have a full $20 million deduction against his remaining income or estate taxes. Thus he manages to escape paying taxes on a significant portion of his fortune.

The establishment of a *family foundation* is important in the task of consolidating family control of accumulated business enterprises, while escaping onerous taxation. This device has become increasingly popular. The number of foundations is growing today at a rate of upwards of two thousand a year for a grand total in the U.S. of over twenty-six thousand, 92 percent having been founded in the last three decades. The significance of this trend is revealed by studying the assets of some of the better-known foundations.[6]

In 1964, $553 million of the Rockefeller Foundation's $862 million in assets were in six oil companies, including 45 percent of the stock of Standard Oil of New Jersey (Exxon). Similarly, $476 million of the

Duke Endowment's $596 million were in the Duke Power Company, $414 million of the Kellogg Foundation's $461 million in Kellogg Company stock (giving it a 51 percent voting majority), and $346 million of the Hartford Foundation's $397 million were held in the Great Atlantic and Pacific Tea Company's stock (ensuring effective control). Perhaps boldest of all these consolidations of business control was Howard Hughes' gift of $500 million in Hughes Aircraft Company stock to the Howard Hughes Medical Institute of Miami, while making himself its *sole trustee*.

This sheltering of corporate profits from taxes by creating a foundation and then placing family and friends on the foundation board in order to assure its availability for corporate advantage is not at all unique. Of fifteen Duke endowment trustees, nine have had associations with the Duke Power Company, and of the six directors of the Lilly Endowment—the third largest foundation in the world—three were officials of the Lilly Company, and three were members of the Lilly family. Similar examples could be extended indefinitely. What is the reason for all this? It protects family ownership, while providing generous tax shelter. Thus S. H. Kress and Co. was able to prevent a takeover bid by Genesco because the Kress Foundation held 42 percent of its voting stock. Or again, the one-third holding of the Hartford Foundation was decisive in heading off a critical move against the present directors of A & P food stores.

This whole foundation game has been summed up quite well by the Stock Exchange firm of Paine, Webber, Jackson, and Curtis. In its publication, *Charitable Foundations,* they point out:

> Since the charitable foundation may remain under the direction of the creator either directly or indirectly, its assets may be used to complement the general financial activities of the creator while still achieving specific desirable charitable goals.[7]

To sum up, (1) capital gains savings through charitable deductions, (2) gifts to family members while living, (3) the marital deduction for surviving wife, (4) business-wise use of family foundations—the result of all of this upon the management of family wealth has been stated clearly by *Fortune* magazine: "Uncle Sam *isn't* taking the big estates."[8]

Still, the art of preserving wealth is only in part the successful escape from estate taxation. The other part must deal with sheltering the ongoing accumulation of wealth from the annual income tax and taxes on corporations.

Shortly before he was assassinated in 1968, Senator Robert Kennedy began to develop a new presidential campaign issue. He uncovered the startling evidence that a number of millionaires and several billion-dollar corporations had paid no income or corporate taxes the preceding year or two. From statistics revealed since that time, it is now evident that the senator had located just the tip of what was in fact an iceberg of taxation escape.

In 1970 (after the 1969 tax reform act) Congressman Henry S. Reuss discovered that 394 individuals with adjusted gross incomes over $100,000 paid no tax. That same year, another 318 individuals paid a minimum tax which Reuss discovered averaged 3 percent for those in the $100,000 to $500,000 income level, 4.42 percent for the $500,000 to $1 million a year persons, and 3.95 percent for those above $1 million.[9] Statistics show that the number of very wealthy individuals paying no or extremely low-rate taxes has steadily increased over the past several years.

This same tax pattern can be seen in the practice of corporate taxation. Using figures from 1971, we find the following:[10]

Corporation	Year's Income (Net Profit Before Taxes:)	Percent of Income Paid in Taxes:
ITT	$ 413,858,000	5%
Alco Aluminum	50,199,000	.0%
Standard Oil (Calif.)	855,692,000	1.6%
Gulf Oil	1,324,914,000	2.3%
Continental Oil	109,030,000	.0%

We could continue this list at much greater length. But the point is already clear. Certain very wealthy persons and certain very lucrative businesses are making off with huge tax benefits.

At this point we will want to ask ourselves two important questions. First, what are the loopholes in income and corporate tax laws that allow this? And, second, is there an interlock between wealthy individuals and ownership of multimillion-dollar corporations that utilize these tax benefits? That is, is there a concentration of special tax privileges at the very top of both our income and our business pyramids? If the answer is yes, the implications for a self-proclaimed "free-enterprise" system are ominous, for the rest of us personal and business taxpayers pick up the check for these privileges and thus execute our own financial undermining.

Harvard University's Stanley Surrey, a past assistant secretary for Tax Policy in the U.S. Treasury Department, has listed major tax loopholes in the order of the amount of money that escapes each year from the overall tax system. They are:

1. the excluded half of capital gains
2. interest on state and local bonds
3. deductions of unlimited charitable contributions
4. farm "tax losses"
5. percentage depletion in excess of basis
6. deductions for intangible drilling expenses[11]

Who are the users of these big tax benefits? The following chart shows the situation in 1972 as regards the two top loopholes in the above list.[12]

Income Bracket	Capital Gains Preference (in millions)	Exemption of Interest on State and Local Debt (in millions)
$ 7,000–$10,000	190	5
10,000– 15,000	340	10
15,000– 20,000	340	25
20,000– 50,000	1,260	125
50,000–100,000	1,080	375
over $100,000	3,580	455

The top 10 percent of our population—roughly families making *over $20,000*—enjoy the overwhelming proportion of big tax breaks, while the top ½ to 1 percent or less enjoy nearly three times the amount of tax advantage of even the relatively privileged $20,000 to $50,000 group! When you figure how small a group that ½ of 1 percent is, the tax-loophole income per individual wealth owner is immense. A continuous supply of publicly underwritten discretionary income flows to the wealthy few, income that can be used for the further consolidation of their personal fortune, power, and status.

But what of corporate taxes? Does the pattern of tax breaks for individuals interlock at the level of ownership between privileged persons and privileged businesses?

The Geography of Corporate Privilege

This question of an interlock between tax-privileged persons and tax-privileged businesses is key. It reflects upon the question of who rules America, and for whose benefit. Is there a ruling elite at the top of our wealth and business pyramids, an elite that is able to use government to write its own interests into such key social indicators as tax laws, at the expense of the rest of us who must pick up the difference?

Statistics show that large stockholders control about 140 out of the top 200 corporations in America today. These top 200 corporations control, in turn, about two-thirds of the total assets of corporations engaged in manufacturing. Many of these giant firms are under the control of major family interest groups. A Wall Street insider, to take one example, has estimated that the following corporations are "under effective control" of the Morgan (Morgan Guarantee Trust) interest group of New York: United States Steel, General Electric, Electric Bond and Share Company, Consolidated Edison Company, AT&T, and the old New York Central Railroad. Such control is exercised through holding companies, family trusts, and family foundations,[13] examples of which we could extend to other families, such as the Mellons of Pittsburgh, the DuPonts of Delaware, the Rockefellers and Whitneys of New York, and the Motts (General Motors) and Fords of Detroit.

Note that it is precisely these large corporations that benefit most from the present structure of corporate tax law. In 1969, the 100 largest corporations paid on an average just 27 percent in taxes, while the *smaller corporations paid 44 percent.* This larger burden of taxation is a major reason for the overall loss of market leverage by small firms. Thus, the portion of profits going to smaller businesses (those with assets of less than $1 million) dropped "nearly 45 percent between 1959 and 1970 and fell an additional 4 percent between 1970 and 1971." By contrast, the share of profits going to the 260 largest corporations (companies with assets of more than $1 billion) soared from 28 percent in 1959 to nearly 55 percent in 1971.[14] The large corporations are making more profits and paying less taxes than their small business "competitors."

Profits, tax breaks, large corporate ownership—all these seem to be flowing in one direction: toward the extraordinarily privileged few at the top of our society. This can be further illustrated in the very important interlocking of boards of directors of the largest commercials banks and insurance companies. The importance of this relationship lies in the fact that it is banks and insurance companies which are the reservoir of capital used by corporations for reinvestment. "A total of $607 billion, or just under 60 per cent of the $1 trillion of institutional investment in the American economy, is held by commercial banks," with life insurance companies coming in second and supplying an additional 15 percent.[15]

This aggregate of financial power is in the hands of an old boy network that connects the boards of directors of these institutions. Chase Manhattan (the Rockefeller bank), for example, is interlocked with Metropolitan Life, Travelers, Equitable, and New York Life. First National City Bank interlocks with Metropolitan, Prudential, New York Life, and Travelers. Manufacturers Hanover (another New York bank) is interlocked with Prudential, Northwestern Mutual, Travelers, and Mutual Benefit Life.

All of this has caused professor William Domhoff, in his illuminating book *Who Rules America?*, to conclude that "there is a national corporate economy that is run by the same group of several thousand men."[16] He is backed up in this claim by Morton Mintz, who in his *America, Inc.* points out: "Power does not countervail. It attracts. Among the powerful, mutual assistance pacts are less painful than prolonged strife."[17] Lest we miss the implications for those of us who call ourselves average middle Americans, Ralph Nader reminds us of its everyday effect.

> The countervailing power [of big business, big labor unions, and big government] turns out to be mostly an accommodating power which transfers the results of corporate abuses from one point on the market or the environmental and governmental continuum until they land on the point of least resistance—the consumer-citizen-taxpayer.[18]

But why does government not do a better job of protecting us? Why are we average people so underrepresented by those we elect every two, four, or six years to represent us? We are off to a good start in looking for our answer when we notice that forty-six of the one hundred United States senators are millionaires. This fact prompts us to ask: Just what are the personal money interests of our politicians? (Our examples will be drawn mostly from the House of Representatives because the Senate has no disclosure rules.)

Big Money and Big Politics

One out of every five congressmen has a personal stake in financial institutions. One survey disclosed that ninety members own stock in banks or savings and loan associations. On the powerful House Ways and Means Committee (where tax laws get written) about one-fourth of the total committee have reported business holdings in banking. Similarly, the House Banking and Currency Committee, which has broad regulatory power over the lending industry, shows more than one-third of the total committee disclosing interests in banks or savings and loan associations. On the Senate side is Russell Long, chairman of the Senate Finance Committee, who has a large financial stake in domestic oil and gas and has resisted through his committee's jurisdiction on tax matters any diminution of the oil industry's favored tax treatment.

The legal profession is second after banking and loan institutions as regards the personal interests of congressmen. Fifty-six members continue to maintain their names on their old law firms, and another nineteen say they still do some firm business. Columnist Jack Anderson, collaborating with the late Drew Pearson, selected fifty typical law firms with partners on Capitol Hill. Of these fifty, they found forty represented banks; thirty-one represented insurance companies; eleven handled gas and oil firms; and ten were retained by real estate interests.[19]

All of this has led to some fascinating geography as to the proximity of corporate headquarters and the offices of their legal counsel. For example, southwestern-based Phillips Petroleum and Ashland Oil found it convenient to take their legal needs to a firm located in Portsmouth, Ohio. The convenience in this case was the fact that one of the Ohio firm's partners is Representative William Harsha, who introduced legislation to reduce oil imports. That the rest of us would have to pay higher prices for gas and heating oil should not, the congressman maintains, reflect adversely upon his dedication to the interests of the common voter of his district.

We may find an even more striking example of this kind of extraordinary business geography in the Travelers Corporation. It holds accounts with law firms found in strategically located places, such as Findley, Ohio; Saginaw, Michigan; and Astoria, Oregon. In each town there is a firm with a partner on Capitol Hill with well-placed committee assignments for the protection and advancement of insurance company interests.

Now we may begin to wonder, we average citizens who must use banks and insurance companies and oil products, just whose interests are being protected by those whom we send to Washington to represent us? We need to have much fuller access than we do to information on the financial interests of our local and federal politicians. The more public power a person wields the more he is legitimately subject to the demand for public disclosure of his personal financial interests. How else are we to know *whom he represents?*

Not only do senators and representatives have business interests of their own, but also they remain enormously dependent upon private wealth for the funding of their reelection bids. In a state of any size, a U.S. Senate seat—even when considered "safe"—can cost, and usually does, upwards of $1 million to defend every six years. A House seat usually costs upwards of $100,000 every two years. With that kind of money needed just for a shooting chance, and the realities of election financing by gifts of established interest groups (up from a total in 1964 of $5.7 million to $17.4 million in 1974), is it any surprise that over 90 percent of incumbent officeholders are returned in average elections? No wonder Congress steadfastly refuses public financing of congressional elections. Incumbents have lucrative private sources unavailable to those who run against them.

Of course the biggest political prize of all, in terms of the solicitation of favors crucial to business success, has been the presidential race. It was here, up to the 1974 law providing for federal funding of presidential elections, that some of the most fascinating financial statistics appeared. They revealed how the mutualities of Big Business and Big Politics were practiced. It was, for example, where significant wealthy families did their most open bidding.

In the 1968 election, with Richard Nixon running against Hubert

Humphrey, 90 percent of all the contributions came from just 1 percent of the population. Pursuing the question of who rules America for whose benefit, we would do well to look more closely at this 1 percent and how during this period they in fact allocated their favors.[20]

Rich Donors' List	Republican	Democrat
Officers and directors of the 25 largest corporations:	$ 699,000	$132,000
Members of 12 prominent families: (total)	2,581,000	150,000
The Rockefellers:	1,701,000	13,500
The Mellons:	279,000	17,000
The Pews:	208,000	—
Officers and directors of the American Petroleum Institute:	429,000	31,000
Individuals with wealth of $150 million or more	1,021,000	106,000
Bankers	478,261	14,493

With the new law on presidential elections, this role of big wealth will have to confine its election interests to the House and Senate. It will not, of course, have to confine its interests in regard to White House appointments and the overall composition of the executive branch.

Looking at the role of big money in the House and Senate races, the one-sided pattern is demonstrated by certain key races. For example, Senator Albert Gore, a long-time critic of corporate mergers and the concentration of energy policy into major oil companies, lost his bid for reelection in 1970. In the primary and general election, Gore's campaign committee spent $500,000. His successful opponent, William Brock, spent more than $2 million. In that same election year liberal Texas Senator Yarborough was defeated by multimillionaire Lloyd Bentsen. A *Washington Post* story later indicated that in the Bentsen versus Yarborough race "oilmen accounted for almost 46 per cent of the individual contributions of $5000 or more. . . . Bankers, investors, mutual fund managers, and others in the financial world [together with these oil men] . . . accounted for slightly less than 65 per cent of the [total contributions]."[21]

There are also less publicly traceable ways in which the owners and managers of large corporations can help out friends in Congress at election time. Corporations can pay cash bonuses to employees with the understanding that a portion is to go to selected candidates for their elections. Companies can loan employees to work in campaigns, or they can loan billboard space rent free to approved candidates. One of the more brazen cases which managed to reach the light of day is found in this 1960 affidavit sworn by J. T. Naylor, then vice-president and chief executive of telecommunications operations for ITT. Naylor swore that another ITT executive came to him and said:

> Hal [Harold S. Geneen, then president and board chairman] and the board have a program that is very important to political protection and business development. Hal has given me a selected list of top executives to contribute to the election campaign. You are down for $1,200. This can be financed for you by the company if necessary. . . . You will be expected to recover the amount by covering it up in your traveling expense account.[22]

This legal and not-so-legal back scratching between big money and big politics has caused Senator Daniel Inouye of Hawaii to speak of a "New Aristocracy." "When the Republic was founded," Senator Inouye pointed out, "the majority of the architects were quite intent on ridding themselves of an aristocracy. I am afraid that realities and practicalities of the election process have, to some extent, developed a new aristocracy of wealth and power."[23] This new aristocracy of wealth and power is vividly exhibited in the personal biographies and patterns of recruitment for top positions in the executive branch of government.

Beginning from the top, in the first half of the twentieth century five out of eight presidents were graduates of such elite universities as Harvard, Yale, Princeton, or Amherst, with a sixth coming from Stanford—the "Harvard" of the West Coast. Of the eight secretaries of state since 1932, five have been members of the Social Register— the prestigious listing of the upper class compiled in several key cities. Or again, of the eight secretaries of defense since that post was created in 1947, five were listed in the Social Register, and the remaining three were a corporation lawyer, a president of General Motors, and a president of Ford Motor Company. Despite lip service about freedom of opportunity, top power in the executive branch has been top-heavy in the recruitment of established patricians.

Moreover, a recent study of the backgrounds and training of non-upper-class federal executives has found that in most cases they were employed in, trained by, and selected from institutions which are both controlled by and primarily benefit the upper class—namely, the major corporations, corporate law firms, large foundations, and elite universities.[24]

Once in place in the higher echelons of the federal bureaucracy, these persons of upper-class standing are given the use of public power to decide between the conflicting interests which come before key administrative agencies. It is not difficult to detect a certain insiders' or old-boy network coming to the surface in this process, a bias for large, established interests—interests which in many cases conflict with those of the average citizen.

The result of all this is that a closed quality has entered into the very heart of the exercise of top political power in our country. Whether by personal financial interest or by the necessities of election costs or by upper-class birth and co-optive training, our society has gotten rather far down the road of oligarchy. It has effectively closed itself against a more open rule by the people. Indeed, as we shall see in a moment, certain important social theorists find nothing to regret in this. It is simply a necessary part, they believe, of the new, post-industrial society. Well, perhaps. But as a way of organizing politics, it certainly is nice financially for those already on top—this intermix of big money and big politics.

The Insider's Game and the Average Man's Interests

Before turning to the ideologues of elitism, we should look at some of the concrete policy results which follow from this closed system of rule. We may begin with a recent example which came to surface in the famous Watergate tapes. It is a discussion between former President Nixon and his special adviser, John Connally of Texas. Secretary of Agriculture Clifford Hardin and Donald Rice, of the Office of Management and Budget, were also present. They were discussing the question of raising milk price supports although the Agriculture Department had advised against it. It involved a promised $2 million election contribution by the Associated Milk Producers, Inc. A key portion of that taped discussion went like this:[25]

CONNALLY: . . . They're [the AMPI] doing some things that I think are a little strong-armed tactics, perhaps, in, uh, the organizing, uh. But, uh, I don't criticize that unless we are prepared to take on business and labor and all at the same time. There's no point in denying the farmer what's the practice for the laborer. And, uh, so I'm not, I wouldn't judge it on a moral basis. I judge it on the basis of, uh—

PRESIDENT: What's the cost?

HARDIN: Oh, it's just a wild guess. They said thirty-five million and I would suggest that it's, uh, nearer a hundred.

PRESIDENT: . . . My political judgment is that the Congress is going to pass it [the milk price support rise]. I could not veto it. Not because they're milkers, but because they're farmers. And it would be just turning down the whole damn middle America . . . under the circumstances, I think the best thing to do is to just, uh, relax and enjoy it. . . .

The president failed to point out that it was the average American consumer-taxpayer who was here getting raped—while big business and big government "relaxed and enjoyed it." It is a classic example of the failure of government to countervail the interest-push of big business. This is but one illustration (it could be almost endlessly duplicated) of the way in which we do not have a system of countervailing power but a system of mutual trade-offs between large, organized interest groups which include, as Mr. Connally said, big labor. The price of this insider's game is paid for not only by average taxpayers, but also by those average workers and businessmen who are not part of the organized interest-group power system. *Numerically, this turns out to be the vast majority of us!*

Perhaps the place where we feel the pinch of all this most plainly, and thus where we may be firmly grasped by its injustice, is in the recent steep rise in the rate of inflation. The combination of profit push and wage push by big business and big labor is not countered, as we have seen, by big government, but simply passed along onto the general economy, and more especially onto those within that economy least able to defend themselves. Thus, while inflation was devastating the average family budget at better than a 12 percent increase in 1973–1974, business profits registered a happy rise of 64 percent in the last quarter of 1973 and first quarter of 1974, with an additional 28 percent in the second quarter. Note carefully that the only part of the American working force able to stay even with this steep rise was the portion lucky enough to be located in the toughest and market-wise most favored unions, or those in advantaged positions in business, law, and medicine.

This fact is illustrated in a set of statistics taken from the period of 1960–1966. Consumer prices increased 14.1 percent over those years. Profits, however, rose 88 percent, or *six times as fast* as prices. This price rise could not be blamed on unit labor costs which in general went up less than 2.5 percent.[26] This latter figure shows concretely how much of the laboring force in fact falls *outside* of cost-of-living protection. Furthermore, the fact that the Democrats held both White House and congressional power during those years points out how poorly even liberal administrations have served the interests of average taxpayers and workers. We have had, for more than a decade now, a *tax and profit inflation* benefiting the advantaged few at the expense of the average many.

The New Explainers

An interesting perspective upon all this can be added by turning our analysis of American wealth and power to a brief examination of the rather remarkable rhetoric of those new social explainers who see in this growth of power by the elite not a threat to democracy, but simply the benign necessity of a post-industrial society.

"The crucial distinction between the world of yesterday and today," writes political scientist Suzanne Keller in her influential book, *Beyond the Ruling Class,* "is that achievement not birth determines social standing, and educational qualifications, skills, experience, and training must be individually achieved."[27] This reputed new equality, an equality of the technically trained and meritorious, is the foundation stone upon which the ruling intellectual consensus presently lays its case. That case, put simply, is that because of the complexities of advanced industrial society, control by an elite of professional managers is inevitable. But this elite control is benign, so the theory goes, because it has gained independence from the old ruling class of wealth, and it is open to all through education. Moreover, the system leaves room for nonelites to gain social leverage through the pressures (1) of elections and (2) of organized interest groups. In this way the new explainers try to reconcile the traditional notions of democracy with the evident elitism of today.

For example, Harold Lasswell argues that "in all large-scale societies the decisions at any given time are typically in the hands of a small number of people."[28] This is even more true under the conditions of advanced capitalist nations where, as economist Robert Heilbroner argues, "new elites based on science and technology are gradually displacing the older elites based on wealth."[29] This thesis of a new elite based on knowledge, but democratically benign because separate from the power of concentrated wealth, is key to Daniel Bell's book, *The Coming of Post-Industrial Society.* "If the dominant figures of the past hundred years have been the entrepreneur, the businessman, and the industrial executive," Bell proclaims, "the 'new men' are the scientists, the mathematicians, the economists, and the engineers of the new intellectual technology."[30]

This, then, is the description of a new democratic elite, recruited supposedly not by class background but on the basis of intellectual merit. It is argued that not only is democracy preserved in this sense, but also the nonelite—the masses—can gain access to social power through elections and through organizing themselves into interest groups to lobby in the pressure system.[31] Beyond this public process of check-and-balance, so the theory goes, is the private system of countervailing *interests* within the competing elites themselves. In Keller's words:

> The postulate of advanced industrial societies being led by a new ruling class sharing a single set of attributes is thus contrary to currently ascertainable trends. Rather, such societies include a number of coexisting pyramids, each with its own internal hierarchy, folklore, rituals, and prizes.[32]

From all of this Bell concludes, and here he speaks for the consensus of the new explainers:

> The decline of inherited power (but not necessarily of wealth) meant that the social upper class of wealthy businessmen and their descendants no longer constituted a ruling class; the rise of the managers meant that there was no continuity of power in the hands of a specific special group. The continuity of power was in the institutional position. Rule was largely in the hands of the technical-intellectual elite, including corporate managers, and the political directorate who occupied the institutional position at the time. Individuals and families pass; the institutional power remains.[33]

In short, elites there may (indeed must) be, but they are democratically recruited and independent of the influence of concentrated wealth. That anyway is the thesis.

What are we to make of this argument? It certainly goes against the documentation we have assembled thus far. If these new explainers are right, then we have been following a path into unwarranted and wasted anger. On the other hand, if they are wrong, these new explainers, then their illusions are important to unmask. For as they stand, they provide an excellent ideological cover for the established way of things, that is, disguising the continuing concentration of money and power behind the fictions of a new meritocracy and a new equality.

When the elite defenders speak of the new knowledge-holders as a "group," or in Bell's case even as a "class," I believe they fail to recognize the degree to which individually the technocrats remain *employees,* easily replaced, and subject to the overall logic of the profit system. Furthermore, successful corporate managers tend to be elevated into ownership through the tax-sheltering device of stock options. Indeed, Adolf Berle, who is quoted favorably by the new explainers for his defense of the idea of the growing separation of power and property, nevertheless concluded elsewhere in that same book (and for democracy more ominously):

> Ultimately, a relatively small oligarchy of men operating in the same atmosphere [Berle believed they would be owners and managers of a few fiduciary institutions], absorbing the same information, moving in the same circles and in a relatively small world knowing each other, dealing with each other, and having more in common than differences, will hold the reins.[34]

Now this sounds very much like the old-boy network discussed earlier. Put this concentration of power together with the evidence already presented that recruitment for the ruling few is less unbiasedly meritorious and more either inherited or by co-optive training, and the whole argument for a democratically benign new elite begins to unravel.

But if the elite is more closed in its constitution and bias than often admitted, what about the nonelite system of countervailing power? Unfortunately, things are no better here. Political scientist E. E. Schattschneider quite accurately concludes:

> The flaw in the [interest-group] pluralist heaven is that the heavenly chorus

sings with a strong upper-class accent. Probably about 90 per cent of the people cannot get into the pressure system.[35]

This is to say that rather than provide entrance for nonelites into the political brokering system, more often than not established interest groups act as guardians at the portals of public power to keep new and potentially competing groups out. They can do this because, as political theorist Peter Bachrach points out, "each elite tends to dominate in its own sphere of activity and to encounter little if any interference or concern from other elites."[36] The so-called pluralist, countervailing system is mostly in practice an accommodating system.

Or again, the evidence we have introduced on the sometimes open, but more often clandestine, interaction between Big Money and Big Politics tends to undermine any secure confidence that the nonelite masses have an effective say through political elections. If they did, I suspect we would have long since had changes in income tax laws, oil depletion allowance, financial disclosure laws, corporate tax loopholes, and so on.

At every point the logic of the new explainers is subject to severe reservations, which raises the question of the function of its continued popularity among a number of well-placed intellectuals. Professor Bachrach has begun to see the forest behind these trees. Namely, it is *the intellectual's suspicion of the "unruly" masses* which here finds sophisticated defense. After all, the job of the professional explainer (i.e., college professors) depends upon the idea that average people need large doses of "training." As Bachrach says,

> All elite theories are founded on two basic assumptions: first, that the masses are inherently incompetent, and second, that they are, at best, pliable, inert stuff or, at worst, aroused, unruly creatures possessing an insatiable proclivity to undermine both culture and liberty.[37]

A journey through recent political theory which claims itself as "realist" reveals a rather shattering undertone of precisely this suspicion of—what was once an honorable phrase—"the people." And where the people are greeted with a paternalistic doubt concerning their competence for self-governance, then already the issue of democracy has been fundamentally settled—negatively.

The realities, as distinguished from the dreams of modern America, seem to indicate a situation of concentrated wealth and power, which is effectively in the saddle of social rule, and more rather than less closed to open recruitment. This reality remains disguised in part because of the rhetoric of the new explainers who argue for a reconciliation between democracy and rule by an intellectual elite. But this elite rule, when examined closely, turns out to be not only less meritocratic but also less democratic in inclination than popularly presented.

In terms of benefit and control, we remain a quite closed system of power. But if we can only be induced to *blame ourselves* for this, then everything remains unchanged. If *we* are the failure, as the theory of social elitism covertly suggests—viz., only experts can manage our incompetences—then we have no grounds for complaint.

4 FAILURE

Social order can reign only if men are content with their lot.

"But what is needed for them to be content, is not that they have more or less but that they be convinced that they have no right to more or less." [1]

—Emil Durkheim

What does it do to the imagination of a person that he or she lives in a society where the head of a business firm can make (and keep) 25 or even 50 times as much as that firm's lowest paid employee? What does it do to the dynamics of hope and self-esteem that a society dominated by a privileged few nevertheless tries to make sense of itself in terms of upward mobility and freedom of opportunity? How do "success" and "failure" work in such a place where we are forced to compete so unequally against each other for our self-respect? We can bring this issue more sharply into focus by asking a still further question.

What happens when a teacher recognizes how steeply pyramided the available hierarchies of success are and then notices at the same time that the grading system turns out few winners but many losers—only 3 A's for every 15 B's, for every 25 C's and so on? What happens when that teacher tumbles upon the suspicion that our society thus begins its fundamental sorting and filing system at an early age—namely, teaching people how to fail without complaint? Do things begin to short-circuit for that teacher?

The teacher may try to rationalize his position by persuading himself that (1) every society must devise a system for allocating scarce, socially advantageous positions; (2) accomplishment in learning is about as good a criterion as any; and (3) our society does in fact allocate advantage on the basis of learning, while our schools do in fact produce learning. Those who argue that government by a new intellectual elite remains essentially democratic would support such a position. But a teacher who can persuade himself to adopt this point of view appears to me deluded. As a result, our educational professions are, or at least should be, in a crisis of conscience.

The engine of American education is the *myth of freedom of opportunity*. It is its fundamental dream. The promise of that myth is what the educational system owns and distributes. It is education's hold on society. Yet the reality is that inherited wealth and advantage remain *the most decisive variables* in the distribution of opportunity and status. And the style of that distribution has not changed significantly in this country in this century—namely, the concentration of wealth and advantage in the top 10, or even 5 percent of our society.

This top 10 percent-or-less group overwhelmingly not only goes to college but graduates from college. More important still, this group has sufficient parental backing to go not just to any college, but to "the right college"—a factor whose importance will increase as a greater proportion of the general population finishes four-year college degrees. Thus, there are systems within the educational system for sorting out relative winners from the really big-time ones. There are, for example, private versus public secondary schools. There are elite Ivy League colleges and graduate schools, and then there are just colleges. Meanwhile, back there behind all this straining and hoping and trying to get A's and B's (rather than C's and D's) from teachers are the better than 85 percent of us who never finish college at all.

So some learn to fail only later on in life. But most learn to fail in our country by the age of fifteen. We spend the major portion of our energy and attention in those early years accomplishing that. As a result, a society of steeply pyramided advantage and wealth is confirmed. This system needs most of us to become failures sooner or later and to blame ourselves for it. As Durkheim saw: ". . . not that they have more or less but that they be convinced that *they have no right to more or less.*"

It would be difficult to think of a more serious accusation to bring against the basic promises that underlie our society—that American education does more to legitimate than to change the fundamental inequality of our country, and that the myth of freedom of opportunity actually functions more to cripple than to make strong. What is the evidence for this charge?

Running with the Young Lions

"The tools of freedom become sources of indignity"—so concluded Sennett and Cobb in their fascinating study of four hundred working-class families in the Boston area. What they discovered was the high degree to which the idea of "getting an education" in order really to move up in life had been internalized by these families. The workers viewed poverty as a combination of (1) material deprivation, and (2) "chaotic, arbitrary, and unpredictable behavior"—i.e., acting *irrationally* and without self-discipline. By way of contrast, those viewed as on their way up were seen as "schooled." They acted rationally, knowingly, dealing with the world "in some controlled, emotionally restrained way"—namely, just the kind of behavior rewarded in an average classroom.[2]

These working-class families accepted education and *educated-type-behavior* as the key to social mobility, even though only 3 to 5 percent of the children from those blue-collar homes make it through four years of college. This situation sets up an interesting tension inside the average classroom—a tension that those of us who are products of the public school system will remember well—the tension between individual accomplishment and fraternity with one's peers.

How often, we remember, it was necessary to play the game of "yeh, I got lucky" in explaining our "A" to our buddies. Time and again we learned to say *"she gave me"* rather than *"I got"* (the grade). For what was going on was a terrible game of shaming and self-doubt; and we had somehow to say "I'm sorry, it's not my fault." But we also had to succeed. And so, in trying to win respect from the figure behind the desk who owned the system, we became part of the denial of self-esteem to the majority. We alienated our peers. They knew that we were on our way. And both they and we knew they were not. So the classroom somehow broke all our hearts a little, and it strangely mixed success with a sense of betrayal. The class-room—it's a rather precise designation for what goes on there. It is the room where we learn our class, our *place* in society. Contrary to what defenders of the new intellectual elite claim, success at education does not teach democracy.

Sennett and Cobb saw the bewilderment of it all. "People usually get involved in such games of aggressive inequality," they said, "not for the pleasure of wounding others, but in order to validate themselves as distinctive, as having respect-able capacities."[3] Later on in life, this contest can shift to a kind of compulsive consuming. It has less to do with gratification of desire than with the pursuit of an old ache, something taking its rise out of a self-doubt we are still trying to resolve. It is less materialism than a restless, disconcerted search of the spirit. That is why we like to live in neighborhoods that feel right, where the standards of pecuniary comparison are not just withering to us. For the terrible thing about inequality in our society is that it sets up a contest for dignity, where most of the time we are so deeply threatened with injury that we must spend enormous energy on convivial or neighborhood modes of protecting our self-esteem.

Earlier in life, the defenses had to do with *labeling:* "teacher's pet," "can't throw a baseball," the guy who's not "a regular guy," the "four-eyed" girl, the shameless "teacher-hustler." Later we learn to deride and yet (in our psychic ambivalence) to fawn upon the antics of the super rich. We sense the game has been fixed; yet we still accept it as *our* game. But it is not; *it's theirs!*

To speak frankly, the instruction of the young lions learning to run the glory road was not really in those *public* school classrooms to begin with. What was being sorted out there was the middle and lower echelons of our society. To talk about wealth owners rather than wage earners, it is necessary to turn to the private secondary schools which are rather nicely called the preparatory schools.

In William Domhoff's *Who Rules America?* the author seeks to establish the idea that in America we have a ruling class composed of the top 0.5 percent of our population. One of the key indicators for membership in this group, he discovered, was attendance at one of the elite preparatory schools. For example, descendants of sixty-five out of the eighty-seven great American fortunes which Myers studied in his *History of the Great American Fortune* turned out to have attended either Groton, St. Paul's, or St. Mark's during the period

1890 to 1940.[4] Graduates of these and other private secondary schools normally go on to one of the elite private universities. We can see this in the class which graduated from the Lawrenceville School (outside of Princeton, New Jersey) in 1965. Here is a list of the colleges and universities which they chose:[5]

14	*Harvard*	5	*Berkeley (University of California)*
10	*Princeton*		
8	*Yale*	4	*Columbia*
7	*Georgetown*	4	*Bucknell*
7	*University of N. Carolina*	4	*Penn*
5	*Brown*	4	*Stanford*
5	*Cornell*	4	*Vanderbilt*
		4	*Wesleyan*

The significance of this one-sided choice of the Ivy League schools is revealed in a recent *Fortune* magazine study which showed that 35 percent of top corporate leadership presently graduate from Ivy League schools. Add to this the 45 percent which come from other *private* colleges, and you can see that this leaves only 20 percent of the management of large corporations coming from our public universities or entering business without having graduated from college.[6]

We can look at this issue of the education of the upper class in another way. A recent poll shows that the prestigious *Social Register* of New York City is composed largely (actually 67 percent of the adult male members) of graduates from Harvard, Yale, or Princeton. In the same vein, a study of 476 top executives who went to college showed that 86 percent of them went to Harvard, Yale, or Princeton.[7] The educational feeding patterns which lead into important business management or corporate law firms—the favorite abodes of the wealthy—are quite strikingly skewed in favor of private secondary schools leading on to prestigious Ivy League colleges.

What students learn in this educational process, clearly, are not simply intellectual skills but skills of social grace. Perhaps most important of all is the early and persistent training in being at the top, of learning to run with the young lions, who will later become the leaders of their respective communities. This is an indispensable instruction in self-confidence in a society where the rest must win their self-assurance rather than have it assumed by birth and background.

Obviously, this is *not* to say that only people from upper-class backgrounds go to private secondary and Ivy League schools. Indeed, one of the social functions of the prestigious private college is to discover the most promising of the nonmoneyed classes and co-opt them into upper-class service. As Domhoff puts it,

> The co-optation of bright young men [sic!] into the American upper class occurs through education at private schools, elite universities, and elite law schools; through success as a corporation executive; through membership in exclusive gentlemen's clubs; and through participation in exclusive charities.[8]

A typical biography might go like this. A bright Italian A-student, from South Philadelphia, let us say, might go to Yale where he becomes friends with important old-moneyed Philadelphia B-students, *for whom*—and perhaps eventually even *with whom*—he later works in top management, finance, or law. Along the way of his climb upwards he will join the Racquet Club in Philadelphia and later, when more proven, be invited into membership at the Union League. He will in turn raise his own children not in South Philadelphia but in suburban St. Davids. And he will send them to private secondary schools in New England for their education. He will, in that sense, have completed his emigration.

But we need to note clearly how *very modest* in numbers is this entrance from below into the upper class. Even if one manages, or more likely one's parents manage, to put oneself into the proper geography for co-option, one's chances of being chosen are slim. The *Fortune* magazine study of business leadership we mentioned earlier showed that:

> only 16 percent are the sons of blue-collar workers or farmers. . . . Forty-five percent of their fathers stood at the very top of the business hierarchy either as founder, chairman, or president of a company, or as a self-employed businessman.[9]

The report also showed that 80 percent of top executives were Protestants. In banking and insurance—the crucial preserves of investment capital—fully 93 percent were Protestants![10]

All of which is to say, we have a majority instructed in failure not only *in* schools (few A's, more B's, and still more C's, etc.), but also *between* schools (private versus public, elite versus nonelite), and finally, too, in the religio-cultural signaling system that maps and directs traffic in the wider society. Taken together, this is the way in which our society has managed its sense of reward and grievance, allocating the degrees of winners and losers. And in this process, education has not changed American society so much as mirrored it. Its task (rather successfully performed) has been to teach people to stay in their place, without complaint except against themselves. American education has been aided in this process by the cultural supremacy of the Anglo-Saxon ideal.

The Protestant Establishment

Thorstein Veblen saw clearly the social function of *manners*. "The value of manners," he pointed out, "lies in the fact that they are the voucher of a life of leisure."[11] By "leisure" Veblen meant not so much that the mannered class did nothing all day; rather it was the style with which they entered into relationship with their peers, displaying a certain relaxedness that is available to those who do not need constantly to pursue and win their self-respect. Taken-for-grantedness of social standing is what gives the Protestant Establishment (remember how few members of Protestant churches this actually involves) their leisured appearance.

E. Digby Baltzell, a sociologist at the University of Pennsylvania, has subjected this small elite to an intensive analysis.[12] He found its members moving through certain typical haunts. He noted, as we have, the connection of caste and campus. Next to this relationship, and perhaps surpassing it in importance, are the ethnically and religiously exclusive gentlemen's clubs. In New York the Knickerbocker and the Links, the Somerset in Boston, the Pacific Union in San Francisco, and the Union League in Philadelphia are examples. As banker J. P. Morgan once said, "You can do business with anyone, but only sail with a gentleman." Better yet, do both with gentlemen, who can be found each day at one's club. Thus, out of the twenty largest corporations in the country at least one member from the board of directors of twelve is a member of the Links Club in New York. Prominent are General Electric with seven, Chrysler with four, Westinghouse with four, IBM with three, and U. S. Steel with two. Baltzell sees what is involved here in terms of the distribution of business power and advantage in actual practice. He points out:

> The growth of the large corporation had inadvertently produced somewhat of a caste situation in which the national corporations were run by managers chosen on a merit system, which actually meant that they possessed the proper college, ethnic and club affiliations, while, at the same time, the objective criteria of survival in a free market tended to test primarily the marginal, ethnic entrepreneurs, among the most successful of whom were Jews.[13]

The system of American achievement is to pass the scramble downwards, deflecting competition upon one's inferiors, especially one's "religious inferiors."

Besides colleges and clubs, the debutante ball is important to upper-class society as a means by which to corral what otherwise might become disruptive, adolescent libido. As Baltzell put it, "Their parents made sure that the democratic whims of romantic love were focused on the 'right' boys from their own caste backgrounds."[14] This same purpose is served by attendance at exclusive summer resorts. Witness *Time* magazine of July 2, 1965:

> Today, Nathan Pusey [then President of Harvard], Walter Lippmann, Thomas Gates [one-time Secretary of Defense], and Nelson Rockefeller go there [Mount Desert, Maine] to relax and enjoy some of the world's best sailing, with the major derivation of the visitors remaining Boston and Philadelphia.[15]

It was at Mount Desert that the grandson of Joseph Pulitzer (St. Louis) met and eventually married a granddaughter of Samuel Vanclain, former president of Baldwin Locomotive Works. It was there that the granddaughter of George Roberts of the Pennsylvania Railroad met her husband-to-be (for a while), Nelson Rockefeller; and Louise De Koven Bowen, descendant of an old Bar Harborite family from Chicago, met and later married young John Wanamaker of the Philadelphia department store family.

The right schools and clubs, the proper summer and winter resorts, the appropriate charities, such as art museums and symphonies, participation in such upper-class sports as the fox hunt and yachting—these are the outward trappings, and sometimes instruments, of the remarkable inner cohesion of the Protestant Establishment. But more than style of leisured living is involved. Behind these externals lies a style of personality, a prized set of behavioral traits which author Michael Novak has called the Anglo-Saxon Ideal. "America never was a democracy of full political participation by its people," Novak claims. "It has always been a highly structured, authoritarian, conformist, heresy-hunting, company-run network of cities, towns, and rural areas."[16] And presiding over this closed system has been the WASP, driven by, and driving others by, the Anglo-Saxon Ideal.

The virtues prized in this ideal tend toward self-reliance, rational abstractness, and purely functional relatedness. These are in sharp contrast to what Novak sees as the "Ethnic Ideal," which encourages loyalty and honor as the basis of relations, and family dependence and obedience more than individual autonomy. The Americanizing process, therefore, requires at bottom a kind of ethnic deculturation. For an aspiring ethnic, it means learning to become solitary (like a Protestant, alone before his God, bereft of comforting ritual). It means learning to run in the marketplace of success with little compunction about what fraternal loyalties are broken, or simply left behind along the way. In this sense, Americanization teaches persons to be ashamed and embarrassed about the density and thickness of their family past which inhibits the broken-field running required for the marketplace. The result is a process of *shaming,* which Novak sees as a kind of self-conscious attempt by the Protestant Establishment to suppress the past and self-esteem of others, and so make others chase after them as ideals.

Perhaps Novak attributes too much self-conscious manipulation to the WASP establishment. It does not in fact have to be that directly intended. Where the religio-cultural style is combined with steeply unequal patterns of advantage, then automatically the personal presentment and behavioral patterns of the wealthy become invidious comparisons for the many, instruments of their psychic putdown. Inequality, more than the content of the differing cultural ideals, is the problem here. There is also a gentlemanly bias on the part of those whose relative isolation and unself-critical social power tend toward a certain casualness in dealing with the lives of others. *The Great Gatsby,* by F. Scott Fitzgerald, vividly portrays this. The author records:

> They were a careless people, Tom and Daisy—they smashed up things and creatures and then retreated back into their money or their vast

carelessness, or whatever it was that kept them together, and let other people clean up the mess they had made.[17]

The Protestant Establishment, not because it is Protestant but because it is a securely established enclave of inordinate privilege, sets the definition of success in our society, where most must fail quietly. If the result is a kind of psychic wasteland for the many, the cause is not so much the personal animosity of the wealthy as the overall system of repute which maps our society. The wasteland results from, in short, our belief in freedom of opportunity as the underlying cause of a person's social place. The irony is immense. The reputedly *open society* becomes a *wide-open society* where each seeks to establish his preeminence over the other and so has no right to complain about the casualties of the endless stampede.

The Idea of Freedom of Opportunity

After referring to the statistics which record the steep inequality of wealth in our country, political scientist John Schaar points out a simple and shattering truth. He concludes,

> There is no evidence, in the form of major political movements or public policies, that this distribution shocks the American democratic conscience—a fact suggesting that the American conscience on this matter simply is not democratic. . . .[18]

Put another way, experience has shown that one can depend upon middle-class persons to take out their frustration and sense of grievance upon themselves or upon those running alongside or behind them. Many times in this book we have moved into these puzzles, trying to dispel the enthralling myths which deflect our grasp upon reality. Now we come to what may be the heart of the issue. And that is the deep hold the idea of freedom of opportunity has on the social imagination of Americans—working class and managers, hard hat and intellectual. The irony is it is an idea that defines most of us as relative failures—demeaned persons living in a demeaning society. For there is an immense short circuit hidden at the center of the idea of freedom of opportunity.

It is not just the fact that we do not have much equal opportunity, that we have instead a quite closed system of distributing advantage. If that were the only problem, then it would be enough to change the tax and estate laws and the procedures of public elections—things which I think should be done—truly to open up the system of opportunity. *But going this far only takes us halfway.* For throughout our previous analysis there has been another, even deeper level of haunting that moves through our society—in our religion, in our education, and in family discourse between generations. And that is our preoccupation with *success*. We cannot simply *be* who we are, but we *must prove* who we are. We are never quite "at home" with ourselves, but only with what we hope we may become.

Perennial discontent is the un-talked-about fruit of a society which seeks to hold itself together on the basis of the idea of equal opportunity, as the Land of Promise. Only it is a promise that puts everyone endlessly on the run—in a time when the limits of endless expansion are now becoming clearly evident.

In a society whose central myth of meaning is freedom of opportunity, one's value as a person comes to depend upon how well one has accomplished that central social task—*using opportunity.* Thus the struggle for competitive advantage becomes the primary enactment of personal and collective meaning. It sets up a terrible contest for dignity, where we establish our own worth only by outpointing others in the crowded marketplace of respect. Because the market is open-ended and indeterminate, we are always on the run after some new achievement, always pursued by self-doubt. Every level of accomplishment becomes but a new staging area for further achievement. De Tocqueville sensed this curious driven quality of people in our country, "forever brooding over advantages they do not possess." He spoke of a "strange melancholy," a "vague dread," a nagging "disquietude." "In the United States," he said,

> a man builds a house in which to spend his old age, and he sells it before the roof is on; he plants a garden and lets it just as the trees are coming into bearing; he brings a field into tillage and leaves other men to gather the crops; he embraces a profession and gives it up; he settles in a place, which he soon afterwards leaves to carry his changeable longings elsewhere. If his private affairs leave him any leisure, he instantly plunges into the vortex of politics; and if at the end of a year of unremitting labor he finds he has a few days' vacation, his eager curiosity whirls him over the vast extent of the United States, and he will travel fifteen hundred miles in a few days to shake off his happiness. Death at length overtakes him, but it is before he is weary of his bootless chase of that complete felicity which forever escapes him.[19]

Freedom of opportunity transforms those who seek to live and measure themselves by it into an endless restlessness, endlessly pursuing themselves in the marketplace of self-worth. "The striver," as Garry Wills has seen, "can never stop striving." He can never quite catch up to himself, never securely prove himself to himself or others. In that sense he has no place where he is at home. He's always moving, hoping—worrying.[20]

Moreover, the idea of freedom of opportunity, although it seems a liberalizing notion, plays a fundamentally conservative role in society. It tends to transform social criticism into self-criticism, the drive for social change into a passion for self-improvement. This accounts for the popularity of personal growth groups. Equality of opportunity, as John Schaar has seen, "encourages change and growth, to be sure, but mainly along the lines of tendency already apparent and approved in a given society."[21] It sets loose a fervor and struggle which inflate and billow the economy and buoy even further into the heights of advantage those who sit on top of the gigantic, wheezing and puffing machine. The cry of equal opportunity becomes by curious reversal the generator of more effective power at the top.

Because the idea of freedom of opportunity depends upon a free market to establish comparative value, the question of how men should be treated is removed from the realm of human responsibility and decision. Thus, we have the notion of an automatic, post-moral society, analyzed and adjusted by value-free social scientists and social administrators. Any radical social critique is muted into a kind of higher sophistication, which knows it is not "morally competent" to judge what another man's reward should be, and so leaves the reward to the hidden hand of the market to negotiate. This whole approach unburdens the conscience of those who in climbing the ladder of success step on the fingers of those beneath them. Moral suspicion is turned upside down. Now it is those below who need to explain themselves.

Freedom of opportunity as a myth of social meaning produces an endlessly restless civilization whose citizens, when wondering why things are not better after all these years, and even generations, of struggling upward, turn their accusations upon themselves or those below. The immense irony is that "equality of opportunity" becomes the almost impenetrable mask for the pursuit of massive, systematic inequality. It produces a society which cannot understand itself without first stepping outside its own most fundamental promise—the promise that "you, too, can become a winner!"

Education then, has not changed American society as much as mirrored it. Its major function has been to produce a mask of legitimacy for a society where most people turn up losers. Rather than an entrance into freedom of opportunity and upward mobility, education's chief role has been to manufacture a majority sorted and filed from an early age into various degrees of failure, for this is what a country where real advantage and power are sharply concentrated and frozen at the top requires. Education's minor function, for the few who have used its ladder well, has been instruction in an uprootedness from cultural past and peer groups that turns the talented into successfully competing *individuals*—the celebrated intellectual elite or technocrats—whose chief proven virtue is a certain knack at single-minded performance before those who sit behind the desk and own the system. Which is to say, education's highest achievement has been to produce good servants—but lonely people.

Strategies for Survival in the Lonely Society

Tutored and trained in the myths of public meaning in America, we come to inhabit an immense loneliness. We are doubly lonely. We are lonely before each other and lonely within ourselves. Students all our lives of "class-room" running, we perfect a bewitched Midas touch that transforms companions into competitors and changes our external boastful parading into a hidden, private pleading. Schaar puts this double estrangement quite nicely.

> The operative doctrine specifies success as the test of personal worth, and by success is meant victory in the struggle against others for the prizes of wealth and status. The person who enters wholeheartedly into this contest comes to look upon himself as an object or commodity whose value is set, not by his own internal standards of worth but by the valuations others place on the position he occupies.[22]

This is a devastating insight into the human indignity visited upon us, ironically, by our society's highest ideals. We are deprived of community by the pursuit of freedom of opportunity. And we are deprived of a sense of centeredness in a self whose worth is neither product of nor subject to the marketplace of respect.

The massiveness of this assault is revealed by the amount of energy we spend, evidently because we need to, on *convivial forms of self-defense*. Thus, a little analyzed function of our preoccupation with sports is that it provides a system of admiration which is an alternate to the indignities suffered in reflecting upon oneself in the wealth/status marketplace. Sports provide an alternate system of identification with strivers and winners who do not remind us of our own daily defeat. Or there are those neighborhood bars which perform as a kind of halfway house, where complaints can be filed with ready approval and communal support against those judging places called work and wife. Close attention to such places reveals a rather elaborate set of rituals for fraternal comfort and reaffirmation. Or there is the system of gossip among secretaries, where the boss can be ridiculed and shamed, and so the tables turned on the routine put-down inflicted by his patronization and paycheck. Still again, there is that blue-collar sense of pride—too edgy to be very sure of itself—that "we know what it means to do a day's work." Such pride is a shaky declaration of self-worth against the marketplace indignities. And there are the uncounted daydreams while on the job, of trout streams and of the clean and rugged outdoor life, a place "where a man's his own boss" and can fraternize with friends.

These are the hiding places, so to speak, in our society from that hard taskmaster of the emulative ethic. The daily, enormous pouring forth of human energy in the task of self-defense says a great deal about the human price of living our American way of life.

The same may be said of urban political machines and certain unions. They also play a role in personalizing everyday life and taking out of it some of its individualized lonely road running. There is, for example, a leader to whom one relates on the basis of loyalty and mutual recognition rather than marketplace calculation. There is a system of patronage and favors rather than an abstract system of equal opportunity. There is an ethic of "we take care of our own" which provides a measure of relief from the wider marketplace where each man must pursue his own shelter alone.

Uncritically, reformers would tear out all this network of human relatedness and replace it with a more rational—i.e., abstract and bureaucratically neutral—form of human interaction. It is surely no accident that many of these reformers are products of an impressive climb through academic classrooms, where their achievement at the emulative system of self-validation was such that they did not notice how others around them had to scramble for cover.

Indeed, academic professionals in general tend to conceive of the lonely society in an equally lonely way. One becomes recognized as a hard-nosed and practical social interpreter when one applies to the political situation a single-minded calculus of interest-group push and shove. Politics now appears as just another aspect of the struggle for competitive advantage. Men vie with each other for public power in order to protect and advance their private power. There is no sense here of a shared comradeship of civilization, of mutually participating in funding and building up the common life, whose qualities and values inevitably shape our everyday living. Rather, society is viewed as a kind of perpetual-motion machine, a place to run through and do combat in, but not a dwelling place. Thus, the highest political admonition becomes "Get in, or get took!"—the politics of loneliness, of the pursued and the pursuing.

The flaw in this explanation, mostly ignored by academic explainers, is that it in fact takes society for granted. Such social analysis cannot focus upon the underlying bonds of allegiance, of faithfulness to shared myths of social meaning, which are at the heart of how we become citizens of a civilization. It does not identify or take into account that fundamental fuel by which we lend society our lives and hopes and even our children. Thus a good deal of what passes for political realism is insufficiently realistic. It cannot transcend our collective myths or bring them into critical reappraisal. It can only move around inside of them.

The loneliness of the lonely society goes largely without critical analysis, although all around us are these millions of people daily scrambling for cover and devising means of comfort. The convivial modes of self-defense briefly mentioned here point to realities too often ignored. Their existence documents the degree of failure in our society of reputed success and gives us, as we shall see in chapter 6, significant clues for our social reconstruction.

Freedom of opportunity fails as an adequate myth of social meaning not simply because in practice we are denied equality by means of a system of concentrated wealth and power. It fails finally because in assigning personal worth on the basis of competitive merit, it turns us into a nation of competitors. We remain always on the run, trying to win the favor of the person who sits behind the desk and passes out the grades. What we must learn to do instead is to inquire into the criteria for assigning particular grades in the first place, who gets hurt and who gets helped, and whether there are not major areas in society where grading, as such, simply does not belong. In short, we must move beyond individual achievement to community.

Beyond Failure

The opposite of failure is not success but greater equality. We have seen how an achievement-oriented society produces, ironically, a massive degree of weakened self-respect. To get *beyond* failure, we need a society more equal than that equality which is worked out under the method of freedom of opportunity, the equal chance to run against each other. For the kinds of things which get counted as meritorious under that system are too narrow. High grades go to aggressiveness and competitiveness. The capacity to comfort or to provide settings of convivial relaxation is viewed as strictly extracurricular to society's system of objective rewards. Yet there is a good deal of evidence that the latter capacities are of greater benefit to society than the former. We give high grades to mobility and then wonder why our suburbs are so lonely. The arts of neighborhooding remain almost without discussion in our universities and government. We tend, as it were, to count as meritorious activity that which honors the teacher: "To go up, go along." And thus we build into the interiors of our business and educational hierarchies the blindness and inefficiency of obsequious modes of association.

So much have we internalized the narrow focus of what our society regards as praiseworthy behavior that just to raise the issue of a wider system of social grading brings to awareness things we usually walk by unnoticed. Why, we even tend to mark our spiritual leaders—our ministers, priests, and rabbis—on the basis of their entrepreneurial skills in expanding the dimensions of their marketplace repute. Freedom of opportunity, as a central myth of social meaning, seems to have this shriveling effect upon us as a people and society. That is why John Schaar argues:

We need a social order that permits a much greater variety of games. Such a social order could, I think, be based on an effort to find a place for the greatest possible range of natural abilities among men. The variety of available natural abilities is enormous and worth much more exploration than any of the currently dominant conceptions of social order are willing to undertake.[23]

This is surely one of the great circuits that lies at the heart of our our educational enterprise, which owns and distributes this business of freedom of opportunity. Rather than expand persons, it makes them smaller, grading them on a single system of merit. That is why the transcription of equality into equality of opportunity is educationally and socially insufficient. We need, instead, a great deal more talk about fundamental *fairness*.

Fairness has to do with the recognition that a person's worth should not depend, in any final way, upon an emulative system of self-validation. Rather, it relates to the perspective of an inalienable mystery and immensity of memory and meaning that clings to each person, and it cannot be reduced to an outside or alien basis of comparison. Fairness takes its rise from this sense of an original equality among persons, an *equality of being,* which is not subject to the measurement of personal "achievement." Fairness is not in contradiction to competition as such, for it recognizes that some competition can help expand us. But it modifies all modes of competition by perceiving the ultimate foolishness of trying to prove oneself by overcoming others along the way. Such a mad stampede is humanly poverty-stricken and poverty-producing. It reduces us before each other to those who are infinitely calculating, unable to afford and so repressing our curiosity and generousness of spirit.

Furthermore, the kind of buccaneer personality that is encouraged by the myth of freedom of opportunity—learning the arts of running rather than of dwelling—may be functional as long as the basic social need is to expand and energize the marketplace. But what happens if this kind of wide-open society begins to run into fundamental limits—limits to the costs of raw material and energy, limits in terms of environmental pollution and our endless ability to live under the threat of defeat either of ourselves or of our competitors? What happens when the arts of householding need building up, with their values of mutual respect and equal belonging?

Once again, fairness becomes crucial if we are to learn how to live with each other rather than just running against each other. Fairness in society would encourage us to slow down our mad dash for repute by raising the floor of socially guaranteed, basic decency—and so take some of the panic out of middle-class breadwinning. It would pay for this not by further bloating the economy but by lowering the ceiling of inordinate advantage, through income and wealth redistribution, and so removing the sting of invidious comparison. As human persons, we relate to ourselves in terms of the geography of social relatedness encouraged by our society. To become bigger persons, with greater trust and expansion of our abilities, we must move beyond the day-by-day impoverishment of the marketplace race and its freedom of opportunity ideal.

Similarly, as a human species that must now relate self-consciously to the limits of our natural environment (shaped in part by the world-political order), we need a more fair and equal society in order to slow down the mad pace of our acquisitive ethos. We must blunt the compulsion to prove ourselves by outpointing others.

A society where the parameters of wealth and the perception of relative deprivation are more narrowly drawn—with a higher floor of decency and a lower ceiling of dreams—is the effective social means to *take us all beyond failure* as persons and as a species. But to be grasped by this possibility is to lay hold of a new dream, and this means fully exposing the illusions of the old. We shall complete our efforts at this task in the next chapter and then go on to the plan and politics of our needed social change.

5   SUCCESS

"There is no question that riches should be the portion of the godly rather than the wicked, for godliness hath the promise in this life as well as the life to come." [1]

—John Calvin

For all his theoretical enthusiasm about the combining of both earthly and heavenly rewards, John Calvin remained skeptical about the actual practice of wealth getting. After all, the Bible does say something about it being "harder for a rich man to get into heaven than for a camel to pass through the eye of a needle." But by the time of Russell Conwell—popular turn-of-the-century Philadelphia preacher—this healthy skepticism had become transformed into an undisciplined fawning upon the super successful. "Why is it Mr. Carnegie is criticised so sharply by an envious world!" asked Conwell in his "Acres of Diamonds" speech that established his national reputation and through which, according to one enthusiastic biographer, thousands achieved success out of failure. "Because," the preacher concluded, "he has gotten *more* than we." [2]

Envy of those who have more, Conwell asserted, is doubly unfair. It is unfair both because poverty is to be shunned and because wealth is to be emulated. ". . . the number of poor who are to be sympathized with is very small," Conwell intoned. "To sympathize with a man whom God has punished for his sins . . . is to do wrong. . . . there is not a poor person in the United States who was not made poor by his own shortcomings. . . ." [3] And who is to be praised even as the poor are condemned? "I say you ought to be rich; you have no right to be poor. ... This is a wonderfully great life, and you ought to spend your time getting money, because of the power there is in money."[4] Amazing alchemy! Now it's poverty whose financial situation offers doubt as to moral rectitude, while gain becomes proof of piety.

This reversal of the Bible's suspicion about the ways of wealth, if sociologist Max Weber is correct, was wrought through the slow corrupting of the Protestant ethic put to work bolstering the capitalist spirit. Beginning in the admonition of a this-worldly asceticism (no self-indulgence, hard work, etc.), the Protestant ethic ended in an anxious search for signs of personal election among the balance sheets of one's business enterprise. Thus, this-worldly "monks" were forever reinvesting their profits and piling up huge fortunes, so that, at last, Methodist John Wesley had to advise Christians "to gain all they can, and to save all they can." Then by giving all they could, their virtue would be proven.[5]

Nevertheless, this undisciplined awe of success had much to do with the peculiar *sociological* factors of late nineteenth-century America—namely, the integration of millions of immigrant poor into our nation at the very time when industrialization was skyrocketing a few buccaneer businessmen into unimagined heights of wealth. The American Dream came true for the few, while for the many it came to be, if not their reality, then their persistent hope. The gospel of success became the American Gospel because for many of us it was our country's fundamental promise—the chance to make it.

There is little peculiarly Anglo-Saxon in all this and much that is main-line Americana. Those few illustrious examples of that faith's payoff naturally become exemplars of our popular morality. They were subject to religious veneration not simply or even primarily because of the venal ambitions of local parsons, but because in them our national hopes became flesh and walked among us. They reassured the rest of us that we had indeed made the right choice, that we, too, might someday become winners! Russell Conwell spoke for the great American mainstream as he instructed us in that dream which, when believed, *cements us together in this so unequal a place.*

The Gospel of Success

"Now, friends," admonished our instructor in Americana, "there has also come a discouraging gloom upon this country and the laboring men are beginning to feel that they are being held down by a crust over their heads through which they find it impossible to break. . . ."[6] Having raised such unhealthy thoughts concerning the *structures* of wealth and power, Conwell quickly put them to rest. He turned our attention instead to *self-improvement*—and, covertly, to self-blame. ". . . never in the history of our country," he argued, "was there an opportunity so great for the poor man to get rich. . . . The very fact that they get discouraged is what prevents them from getting rich."[7] The problem is *in the self,* not in the structure of power, especially in the self's lack of confidence about itself.

Overcoming discouragement by the techniques of self-confidence building—that is the trick of success. The secret, the power of successful climbing, is to be found *within.*

In putting it that way, Conwell joined his voice to a long line of the gospelers of the American way of rising, a line that stretches down to our own day and its secular, now popular, counterparts. Take an advertisement for "the authoritative guide to Self-Image Modification," a book entitled *Winners and Losers.* The ad appeared in the July, 1974, issue of *Psychology Today* and read (in part):

> With the S.I.M. method you can turn yourself from a loser into a winner! Dr. . . . gives you games, charts, tests, and discussions that will enable you to change your self-image and become what you want to be.[8]

Here is the newest revised version of the old self-improvement mania—*how to* unlock the inner power, release the secret of success within, and find the "acres of diamonds" right in your own backyard. All of this straining and groaning and hoping at personal improvement leaves the great wheezing and puffing machine that is the American Dream unchanged—few winners, many losers, and much dreaming. Moreover, the therapy is endless—these nostrums of self-improvement, this seeking of the trick of release for the energies of self-confidence. It feeds on an endless uncertainty forever seeking a new method, a new book, or a new instructor. That is why it has had such an elaborate history.

Back in 1907, for example, the fashionable Frank Haddock, inspirational author of the famous "Power Book Library," complemented his earlier productions—*Power for Success* and *Business Power*—with a new volume, *Power of Will.* The secret of success is within, he proclaimed. "It is the Will . . . who [sic] should now step forward to take the command. . . ."[9] And how does one accomplish this commanding spirit, this take-charge attitude? Haddock suggested practical exercises, following the right method, the technology of self-confidence. Thus:

> *(a) Exercise No. 10.* Stand erect. Summon a sense of resolution. Throw Will into the act of standing. Absorbed in self, think calmly but with power these words: "I am standing erect. All is well! I am conscious of nothing but good!" Attaining the Mood indicated, walk slowly and deliberately about the room. Do not strut. Be natural, yet encourage a sense of forcefulness. Rest in a chair. Repeat, with rests, fifteen minutes.
>
> *(b)* Repeat every day indefinitely.[10]

This tradition was continued by Chicago businessman William Walker Atkinson, who published *The Secret of Success* in 1908 and *The Psychology of Salesmanship* in 1909—each expounding a method of mind cure and self-confidence building.[11] Or there was Napoleon Hill (author of *The Law of Success* and *How to Sell your Way through Life*), who published his *Think and Grow Rich* in 1937, advocating optimism, diligence, and self-help as the "secret of power" which, according to Hill, Andrew Carnegie had revealed to him years before. Hill preached in true gospel fashion:

> hold your thoughts on . . . money by concentration, or fixation of attention, with your eyes closed, until you can actually see the physical appearance of the money. Do this at least once each day.[12]

The popularity of this book carried it through twenty-eight printings and led to a paperback edition as recently as 1961!

Appropriately enough, Henry Ford himself gave graphic impetus to this line of success technology. Ralph Trine, his biographer, set forth the following transcript of a 1928 conversation with the auto king in his *The Power That Wins.* Trine reports Ford as saying:

> Each is a world in himself—and at the same time a part of all there is; and all—the ALL—is here now. To his center—himself—he is continually attracting little entities—invisible lives—that are building him up. . . .[13]

In order to hasten this accumulation of life force, Henry Ford advocated that food specialists should concentrate on ways of activating our participation in these surrounding energy fields by finding the combination of foods that would help to develop strong willpower.

Inner power, special diets, and mystical energy sources that can be tapped once one knows the secret method—these are the great American mind cure and formula for success, the energizing of self-confidence through inner power and the spirit of calm command. "How to Achieve a Calm Center for Your Life" or "How to Think Your Way to Success," wrote Norman Vincent Peale in his *A Guide to Confident Living*. Peale also wrote:

> In the subconscious God presides with His illimitable power. If you are allowing yourself to be defeated, practice thinking confidently and focus your thoughts on God. This inward power, this power of God within you, is so tremendous that under stress and in crises people can perform the most incredible feats.[14]

Defeat, failure, success, winning—even God!—all are located *within,* within the striving, hoping, and hurting self. The external structures of privilege remain without critical reappraisal. "Be a man, be independent," Russell Conwell urged, and "then shall the laboring man find the road ever open from poverty to wealth."[15] When you consider that the concentration of our country's wealth has not changed substantially in the seventy years between Conwell's time and our own, you can see why these books must always be rewritten, the gospel refurbished by some new technique. There is always the need for endless penance and sorrow, endless devotion and piety. We pick our way upward, one by one, through a traffic jam—into a roadblock.

The *structures* of wealth and advantage give birth to this nagging *self-doubt.* Runners in the social stampede, we never quite believe in ourselves, never securely get ahead of our intimations of defeat. Preacher Conwell, way back when the gospel of success was first coming into vogue, sensed this without understanding it. That is why he said more than he meant in "Acres of Diamonds"—even as Norman Vincent Peale did many years later in his fatherly comforting of the endlessly self-doubting. Conwell ended his famous speech with the tale of *the stutterer,* that hidden nightmare of all those who stand before others and ask for their applause. The stutterer— that shattering exhibition of incompetence, humiliation, and impotence—was transformed by Conwell into a supreme display of his oratory and power. "As soon as he heard his voice, his hand began to go like that, his knees began to tremble, and then he shook all over." [16] The preacher put belittling ridicule into his speech and gesture.

> He coughed and choked and finally came around to look at his manuscript. Then he began again: "Fellow citizens: We—are—we are—we are—we are—We are very happy—we are very happy—. . . . [17]

Conwell imitated weakness and thus transformed humiliation into an illustration of his command and presence, his personal strength. He consummated his control over his quivering congregation by cleverly reminding them of their lingering incompetence and offering them the comfort of his mastery to nestle under. He made them small and himself big—success performing before dependency.

The forlorn irony in this whole gospel of success is that the search for an inner sense of potency is really the search to find an internal substance and reality that confirm us *beyond* the measuring eyes of others. But winning wealth and fortune, the announced purpose of self-confidence building, is a pursuit that leaves us always unfulfilled. We are not cured by the preachers of mind cure. We are only refurbished for a new run, looking always for a new method, hoping for better luck.

Money, Luck, and Violence

Las Vegas is located at the center of the American Dream. The other altar, in addition to Self-improvement, at which we routinely bow as a people is the altar of Lady Luck. We look for that big break, that once-in-a-life-time lucky chance. Have you ever pondered the psychology of the lottery ticket? Of the $2 racetrack bet? We sense that however much we work at our positive thinking about ourselves, still the deck is stacked, and we have to fall into the right trick to beat the stampede. Behind this hopeless hoping there's a certain sense of realism about how it is in America.

The very essence of money is magic—its ability to transform things into their opposites. This is money's inner power, its psychic hold on us, a fact seen clearly by Karl Marx:

> I *am* ugly, but I can buy the most beautiful women for myself. Consequently, I am not *ugly,* for the effect of ugliness, its power to repel, is annulled by money. [18]

The money we have, what we can *pay for,* is what we *are.* British historian R. H. Tawney put this nicely. He said:

So wealth becomes the foundation of public esteem, and the mass of men who labor, but who do not acquire wealth, are thought to be vulgar and meaningless and insignificant compared with the few who acquire wealth by good fortune. . . .[19]

"By good fortune"—yes, *fortune* has this double connotation: the magic both of money and of how it is attained, for money is closer to mystery in the public mind than it is to the mundane (where we just make a living). "Let us assume man to be man," says Marx, "and his relation to the world to be a human one. Then love can only be exchanged for love, trust for trust, etc."[20] But that is not the case where money is exchanged. Now it is not so much we that live as our purchases that live in us. We become them, and they become us—the transformation of things into persons and persons into things.

"What do you do?"

"Which car is yours?"

"Where do you live?"

At a cocktail party the answers to these questions answer the *who* in the question "who are you?" We are what we own. Our possessions are less an extension of us than we are an extension of them.

Money is my glamour. Money is my good name. Money is my luck. Indeed, money has even become religious. It is our society's mysticism, its sense of transcendence. This spiritualization of money can be seen upon the occasions of Christmas and death.

The commercial exploitation of Christmas began in America somewhere around 1890. By 1960, December buying had become nearly 30 percent of the year's total sales in merchandizing. St. Nicholas and Father Christmas, by tradition festive masters of revelry, were transformed into high performance gift bringers. The older folk customs of setting off firecrackers, shooting guns, convivial drinking, and singing in the streets gave way to the single family gathered around a gift-laden tree. Moreover, as advertising critic Hugh Duncan has put it:

> At Christmas time woman herself is transformed. Erotic, romantic, and occupational roles must be replaced by maternal and familial images in December advertising. This strengthens other festive images of the American Christmas Madonna who gives, not her breast, but gifts bought for money.[21]

The symbol of money replaces the older symbol of festive fellowship. On Christmas morning children call their friends to compare consumer accomplishments. Parents, surrounded by presents, bask in the warmth of once more accomplished love. The family celebrates itself through its purchases. Our fundamental form of social exchange—money—bears the Christmas spirit across the land.

But money knows how to mourn as well as celebrate. As recently as 1910, most families insisted on bringing their dead home from hospitals. Funeral parlors were thought to be forlorn substitutes for those who owned no home or had no friends to lend them theirs. The body was laid out by the grieving family or by a neighbor experienced in handling the dead. Friends would arrive in great numbers, bringing pies and cakes and chicken. The religious ceremony was fundamentally familial and neighborly—preceded and followed by the long-practiced arts of convivial comfort among those who had attended each other's griefs before.

Today there is a funeral director, who ushers people through what he has advertised as "the most modern funeral facility in town." The corpse is now "the dearly departed" who is wrapped in a "slumber robe" and taken from the "reposing room" to a "resting place" in a Memorial Garden or a Forest Lawn. Death, like nativity, has become subject to the mystery of money. Respect is shown by elaborate and costly floral arrangements and elegant funereal consumer accomplishments in coffins and limousines. Grief is made public by the purchase of facilities with "elegant reserve," the "dignity" of thick carpets, and the "serenity" of manicured lawns. As Hugh Duncan said,

> Funerals have shifted from churches and homes to commercial funeral homes because spending money in itself has become a way of showing respect, and now in our time, of showing reverence.[22]

Thus money takes on religious significance, not simply as a display of success but as an actual bearer of the transcendent, of the numinous. We are not only devoted to money, but also we express our devotion *through* money. Moreover, our worship is not always mild and middle class. Money comes also to have a strange association with images of violence.

What is this fascination of ours with the children of the rich and the famous who get kidnapped, crippled, or die? What is our collective Las Vegas syndrome that puts together big-time gambling, big-time gangsters, and big-time public interest? What is this inner pilgrimage we take with guns and bank notes and bloody endings? It has to do, I believe, with our love/hate affair with money, our sense both of deprivation and of devotion, and so our desire for revenge. We feel keenly the wounds of our present status. Yet we also love this money that injures us so. And this triggers in us a double violence—both of lust and of injury. Money and violence are woven together in our movies and in our news reports because in them we ventilate our short-circuited desires.

Caught as we are between devotion and deprivation, there is something deeply attractive about the bank robber, the shoot-out, the racket-dominated desert casino, and the playboy racecar driver over the embankment and in flames. Put simply, psychologically *it fits.* Money is our luck, and most of us aren't lucky—ever. So we need to strike back, if only guiltily in our carefully unexamined public lusts.

The Myth of Affluence

This gospel of success, this mystification of money, is a piety that has its parallel in today's world of secular explainers. That parallel is the *myth of affluence*—its grip upon the imagination of many of our most influential social interpreters, and the way this skews their perception of American reality. Abundance has not only a popular but also a sophisticated following. Our analysis of the idea of success requires us to reexamine this myth.

The idea that most Americans enjoy ease and abundance emerged first in the 1950s. It was noted, for example, that for the first time in the history of any society there were in our country more white-collar workers than blue. Such statistics combined nicely with and seemed to confirm the notion that America was coming into a new post-industrial era, with the center of our economic activity moving from industrial production into the service and professional and managerial sectors. America, it was believed, was becoming a nation where the question of economic quantity was being transcended by the majority into an increasing attention to the *quality* of life.

To be sure, a minority of poor remained. But this was seen as a residual problem, needing remedial attention, while the major focus of social concern could appropriately turn to the humanizing use of our new abundance and leisure. Ironically, even as sensitive a social interpreter as Michael Harrington, when talking about "the other America" of the poor or near poor, tended to portray his group (larger, to be sure, than commonly thought) as hidden in the midst of a more general, majoritarian affluence.[23] This is to say that there was no politics to help the poor, but only the moral enthusiasm of the liberal elite.

This notion of average American affluence, it now seems clear, was premature. It was not only premature; it misdirected subsequent efforts at social reform by driving a wedge of "special treatment" between the poor and the middle class. Things were, in fact, much more difficult for the average American family than popular rhetoric let on. But not until some of those earlier statistical indicators of middle-American "affluence" were subject to closer examination did new and quite different interpretive results begin to flow in.

Take, for example, that much heralded movement from a blue- to a white-collar majority. The Census Bureau included in the "White-Collar" classification many persons we would normally think of as working-class: baggagemen, messenger boys, bill collectors, postmen, clerical and sales workers, newsboys, and bus and train dispatchers. Similarly, *excluded* from the list, because they were placed in the "Service" category, were people we would usually think of as blue collarites: janitors, elevator operators, doormen, guards, cooks, household help, barbers, hospital aides, and so on. By correcting the Census Bureau way of sorting job types to reflect more accurately our everyday view of society, we see that something like three-fifths of America today remains working-class. As a group, it averages a modest $9,500 a year per family unit, and 30 percent of them make less than $7,000 a year.

Contrast this to Daniel Bell's picture of what we are becoming as a nation. The emerging "post-industrial society," he says,

> is based on services.... What counts is not raw muscle power or energy but information. The central person is the professional, for he is equipped ... to provide the kinds of skills increasingly in demand ... the services and amenities, health, education, recreation and the arts, which are now deemed desirable and possible for everyone.[24]

This is a happy picture of America for college professors to entertain, because it puts them at the center of things. But the euphoria of Bell's description simply fails to register the fact that forecasts show that even in 1985 only 15 percent of our population will have graduated from college and that the working-class will remain the majority in our society through the end of the century.[25]

We are not only much more *a working-class country* than we have been led to believe, but we are also, most of us, considerably less well off than assumed. Take the "Moderate Family Budget" projected by the Bureau of Labor Statistics which we analyzed in an earlier chapter. Remember that it showed a food budget for a family of four in 1971 of $50 a week, and a housing budget, which must cover mortgage, furnishings, and repair, of $219 a month. Already modest enough, what has often not been noted is that this "moderate budget" presupposed that:

The toaster lasts 23 years.

The refrigerator and stove last 12 years.

The vacuum cleaner is replaced only once every 14 years.

The TV survives 10 years.

The husband buys one year-round suit once every 4 years.

He buys a topcoat once every 8½ years.

The family gets a 2-year-old car and keeps it for 4 years.

The husband takes his wife out to a movie once every 3 months.

The two children go to the movies once every 4 weeks.

And there are no savings.

Is this affluence? Yet, not half the families in this country can attain even this level of living.

The failure to understand that a majority in America remains largely working class and financially struggling has caused certain well-known interpreters of our society to view the middle as essentially comfortable and therefore conservative. As a result, these interpreters turn their hopes for social change to special elites—in the case of John Kenneth Galbraith, to the new technocrats, or for sociologist Philip Slater, to the new commune experimentors, or for the quasi-Marxist Herbert Marcuse, to the few "Great Refusers." Prematurely, I believe, such thinkers have turned their backs on the political potential of a radicalized middle class.

Take Galbraith. "The high production and income," he writes, "which are the fruits of advanced technology and expansive organization remove a very large part of the population from the compulsions and pressures of physical want."[26] But just who are in this "very large part of the population" that Galbraith thinks are so securely comfortable? More than half the families in our country must manage on *less* than the government's moderate budget which depends upon a second-hand car, ancient kitchen facilities, little new clothing, minimal medical and dental bills, and no savings.

As Richard Parker has seen,

> Riesman, Whyte, Galbraith, and many others accepted wholeheartedly the belief that everyone—or nearly everyone—was well-off, that technology was *the* wave of the future . . . and that the New Class [of technocrats], highly educated, fluent in technology and administration, could fine-tune both the economy and the culture in a way that promised to usher in utopia.[27]

The result is that such interpreters turned their hopes for change to an educated elite which had freed itself from wallowing in the foolish acquisitive pursuits of middle-class abundance.

Thus Philip E. Slater, in his widely read book *The Pursuit of Loneliness,* is struck by what he thinks is the central puzzle of modern America: why in the midst of affluence are we persistently haunted by the feeling of scarcity? He concludes that the reason for this contradiction is just that—that it is a *feeling.* Its source is psychological, in the repressed sexuality of middle-class mothers, trapped in emotionally sterile suburbs, off-loading their frustrations and libidinal aridities upon their children (especially male) who thereby receive a massive dose of scarcity feelings—that is, repressed sexuality. The children then translate this psychic bias from the subjective emotional level to the economic, and so fuel the rat race.

Slater has to go through this gymnastics of subtle explanation because he fails to see that much of the running going on in the middle class results from fathers moonlighting or mothers taking part-time jobs. And even then, these families are having to rob Peter to pay Paul for end-of-the-month bills. Both Slater and Galbraith have generalized on the basis of social experiences which are available only to the top 10 percent of our society—that group which makes $25,000 a year or more and routinely sends their children to college.

It is surprising to find Herbert Marcuse joining in this same assumption of affluence. As a New Left quasi-Marxist, his orthodox hope for a different future lies with the working class. But he does not have much hope for them because he thinks the workers in America are too wrapped up in enjoying the good life made possible by technology. Marcuse claims in *One-Dimensional Man* that today "there is no ground on which theory and practice, thought and action meet."[28]

Because of technological affluence, Marcuse argues, the socialist hope has been deprived of its concrete foothold in history—the degradation and impoverishment of the worker. The result is a social homogenization, a one-dimensionality where radical social criticism appears increasingly as a kind of mental deformity to those who want only to be left alone to enjoy their boats and campers. Marcuse says,

> This assimilating trend shows forth in the occupational stratification. In the key industrial establishments the "blue collar" work force declines in relation to the "white collar" element; the number of non-production workers increases.[29]

What Marcuse does not see is that many of these new white-collar and service jobs *pay more poorly* than unionized, industrial labor. The fruits of technological abundance he has in mind have been largely reserved for a special class of highly skilled workers (less than 15 percent), middle and upper management, and the professionals. Deprived of a clearer grasp on middle-class economic realities, Marcuse is left with a forlorn "Great Refusal," available, one suspects, mostly to college students, and only then one-by-one. He does not see—*most social interpreters still do not see*—the mass-based potential for significant social change in the alienated average American. To repeat: in 1966, 45 percent of us agreed with the statement that "the rich get richer while the poor get poorer." More recently, *76 percent agree!* There is a new politics of equality out there for those who can learn how to grasp it.

Equality and Dignity

The task of equality can be stated in economic terms. But its real goal has to do with human dignity and the nurture of self-esteem. Only by understanding *the goal* of equality can one transcend the problems of self-contradiction we found in the "freedom of opportunity" ideal.

That our society *is* unequal should by now be evident. And the burden is borne not just by the few who are poor but by the many who are middle. Indeed, inequality is becoming steeper, ironically, by means of those very tools with which Democrats and Republicans alike try to pacify the middle class—viz., expanding the Gross National Product. We can illustrate this by a diagram of our country's wealth shares.[30]

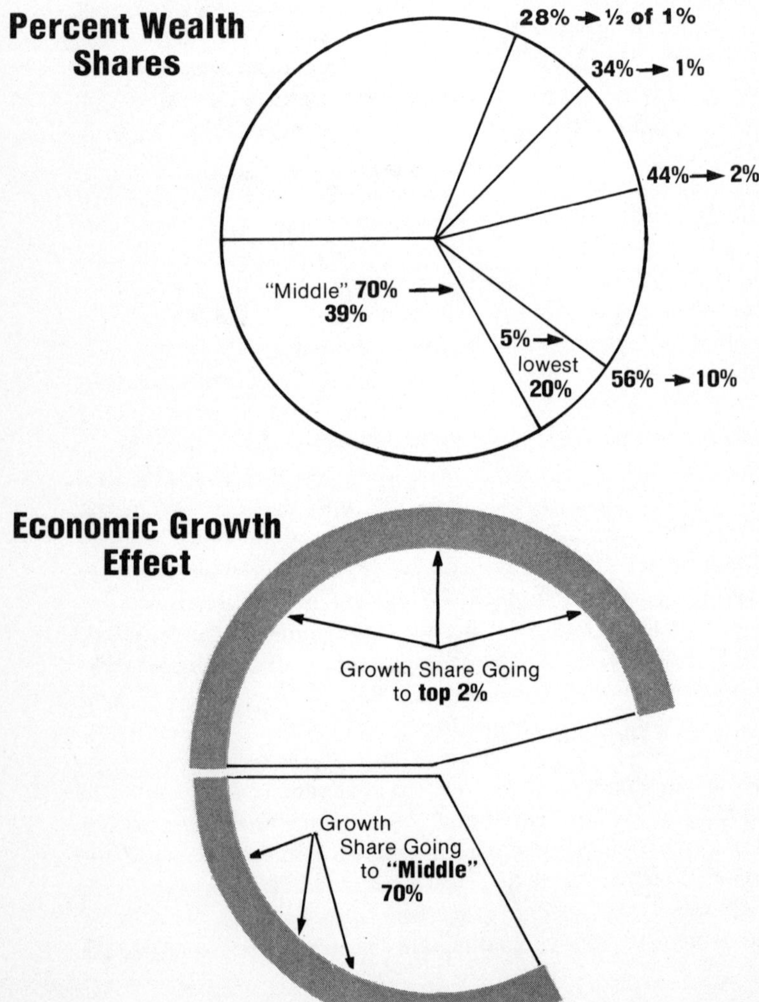

This shows the distribution of wealth in America, where the top ½ of 1 percent of us hold 28 percent of the total personally owned wealth, and where the top 1 percent, 2 percent, and 10 percent own respectively 34 percent, 44 percent, and 56 percent of the wealth. (Meanwhile, the lowest 20 percent of the population owns 5 percent of the wealth.)

The second diagram illustrates another poorly understood fact of our society. The shaded area shows the effect upon the distribution of wealth of an expanding Gross National Product for the top 2 percent of our population. Although relatively small in numbers, this group divides a full 44 percent of the benefits of our overall wealth expansion. Meanwhile, the "middle" 70 percent of us—huge in number—fights over a *smaller,* 39 percent sector.

This second diagram rather nicely illustrates both the mythic and the real effects of an expanding Gross National Product. The *mythic function* of an expanding GNP is to provide the illusion of upward mobility. It makes it possible for average Americans to tell themselves that they are moving up in life and so can be grateful. On the other hand, the *real function* of a growing GNP is to accumulate ever-increasing wealth at the top of our society, wealth which can be used to further the interests of the few and consolidate their power over the many. For example, in 1953 the average size of estate in our country for the top 1.6 percent wealthholders was $186,000. The average estate size for the rest of us, 98.4 percent was $7,900.[31] This comparison is not much different today.

To take the task of equality seriously is to know that one must *change the income shares* going to various groups in our society. Equality requires a redistribution of wealth from the few at the top to the many who are middle and poor. We shall speak of the concrete programs of this transfer in the next chapter. But we should note here that not just greater economic fairness hangs upon this question of redistribution, but so, too, does the future of our dignity as citizens actively participating in the governing of our society.

The goal of equality is not the negative and demeaning one of satisfying our bruised envy. No, the goal of equality, of a more fair society, is to open up the public and its public processes (both political and commercial) to our effective participation as citizens. We gain self-esteem not by endlessly measuring ourselves in the marketplace of equal opportunity where winners and losers are made, but by so ordering the market that each person receives recognition there as a full-fledged participant. Without this interaction with the affairs of public life, a person comes to feel dependent, without anything significant to offer or say, a passive subject of other (i.e., better) people's expertise. However comfortably maintained, such a person feels demeaned, poorly regarded, essentially superfluous. He or she becomes just a *private individual.*

This reduction of the middle class to a passive social role is reflected in our growing preoccupation with purely personal and interpersonal scarcities and satisfactions: personal growth groups, sex therapy, family counseling, transcendental meditation, and so on. Inequality of power has undermined what John Dewey called "genuine publics." The result is that average people are not able to translate their personal problems into public issues and to discuss them at that level. Their world of complaints and enthusiasms is denied the means by which to transcend the interpersonal world and place that world within the wider structures of society. They no longer experience what it means to be a *member* of society, because they find there only persistent reminders of their unimportance. (Occasionally, however, even these private preoccupations can be a kind of protest against the general trivialization of life. They can be a way of beginning to take oneself seriously *again.*)

Ben Wattenberg, in his book *The Real America,* completely ignores this undermining of the middle-class position of social power, and the consequent loss of dignity and a sense of public standing. Wattenberg's citizen is simply a consumer of economic goods and public services. The only inequality Wattenberg is interested in is the income gap between the poor or the once poor and the middle class. He displays no sensitivity to the inequality of power and of status between the average many and the wealthy few at the top of our society—an inequality that is growing. "The evidence of the data," he says, "is the evidence of progress, growth and success."[32] And he concludes that we should think positively about the established way of America and continue to push the mainstream system of distributing accomplishment through extending freedom of opportunity.

But more of the same does not make things better; it makes things more unequal—that is what Wattenberg just doesn't understand. In fact, he doesn't even consider it. He ignores what is in fact the key relationship in our society—that between the average income gainers and the wealth holders of our society. Nor does he focus upon the effect of long-term inflation upon the self-estimate of those who seek to win their self-respect by outpointing others in the display of consumer accomplishment. His "real America" is curiously unreal to anyone who watches our advertising industry and takes seriously what it says about us. In short, Wattenberg shows little grasp on either the power realities or the psychological dynamics of American society.

In happy contrast is Denis Goulet. He achieves a critical reappraisal of just what it might mean for a nation to be "developed." Success requires more than an expanding GNP for the many and sympathetically conceived remedial programs for the few. The successful society has something normatively to do with what people are or can become—with what enhances self-esteem, our sense of personal significance and worthwhile accomplishment. As Goulet puts it, "plentiful goods cannot substitute for the good life."[33] "The American system," he says, "subliminally persuades men to seek status, climb pyramids, and make waste in unrelentingly competitive spirit. Yet competition among unequals breeds domination in the strong and servility in the weak."[34]

The truly developed society displays its development not in things but in its *people*. A successful society is a society which encourages and enhances human dignity, a sense of inner meaning and substance. The development of society is the development of persons as persons, not as consumers, not as fawning second-raters or bleak-hearted winners. From this perspective, Goulet concludes that "The United States constitutes, by and large, an example of anti-development rather than of genuine development."[35] Its buccaneer spirit of commercial rape is a danger both to its own inhabitants and to those in the Third World whose raw materials are expropriated to feed the great eating machine.

The American Dream has served whatever purpose it once had in fueling the wide-open expansion of our economy. A new task spells out our collective future. Its name is not growth, but balance. Its virtues are not those of running, but those of dwelling, of learning to live with each other as members of a common fate. We shall learn this new task, I suspect, not because we want to but because we will have to. Put simply, rapid growth has become too expensive for our means—both economic and ecological, to say nothing of the psychic drain it has all along inflicted.

The real meaning of success, as a person and as a society, is *to be able to be* rather than to have to run. It is to accept ourselves at the place *where we are,* rather than the place we hope someday to be. Success means we can live our everyday reality with dignity rather than through forlorn dreams.

The politics of this kind of success is what we turn to next.

6   CHANGE

"Towards what ultimate point is society tending by its
industrial progress? When the progress ceases, in what
condition are we to expect that it will leave mankind?"[1]
                        —John Stuart Mill, 1857

From the beginning, America has been an unequal country. It is
getting rapidly more so today. The expansion of our economy—that
we have been taught to hope and be grateful for—functions in fact to
transfer discretionary income to the top one percent of our
population, where it is used to buy political favor and to consolidate
social control. Meanwhile we middle many exhaust ourselves and our
pocketbooks by seeking to prove our personal worth by way of
consumer accomplishment and display. We go into debt, feel secretly
panicked, and blame ourselves rather than the system for our plight.
We are told that we have freedom. Yet everywhere we feel unfree,
hemmed in, running without moving. And that feeling accurately
reflects reality.

Our myths of public meaning—that we are middle and mobile and
affluent and enjoy equal opportunity—disguise American realities
and make our pain a puzzle to us. We must disenthrall ourselves in
order to change our circumstances.

That seems more possible today than in the past. Our economy has
entered a time of fundamental contradiction. Given the new situation
in energy, ecology, and basic raw materials, it will cost a lot more in
the future just to maintain the living standard we have already
achieved. As the pie stops becoming larger, people will begin to

wonder how the slices got so disproportionate. A middle-class society in which the curve charting the growth in its standard of living begins to flatten out or even turn downward is in a situation of deep instability.

This makes the present decade a time more ripe for fundamental change than the noisier sixties. The sixties had consciousness-raising and moral enthusiasm but no politics. The majority remained preoccupied with trying to win. Today they know they are not winning. Still, all this could end up just as easily leading only to a more intense quiet desperation, with the competition among the middle many growing ever more brutal. What we have is a *possibility,* a *potential* politics based upon a middle-class sense of grievance. But it is no more than a possibility, and evidence remains ambiguous.

Given that fact, there is at least one other purpose to this book. That is my hope that even if change doesn't come, or is long delayed, some of these insights into the established system of benefit may help those running in the stampede to bring less damaging judgments upon themselves than the prevalent (rigged!) estimate of winners and losers. Knowledge of the social structures can help us shield our self-esteem and make us less vulnerable to the self-undermining which the system as presently constituted encourages. Not economics as such, but the kind of selves our society nurtures is what interests me—the quality of human beings we grow. My own view is that the virtues of learning to live with one another are humanly more ennobling than the arts of cleverly running against each other. Moreover, in our new world of growing resource scarcity, we shall need these capacities for interdependency to survive.

Precisely at this point a complaint can be raised against this book which should be taken seriously. It has to do with the existence of the American economy within the wider poverty of much of the world— the fact that the inequality within our country is dwarfed by the inequality between us and most of the Third World. There are some who might argue that all I have done in fanning the middle-class sense of discontent and relative deprivation is to add psychic fuel to America's continuing rape of the world's resources in its desperate effort to get our Gross National Product rolling again. Rather—such critics might say—we need to persuade the middle class that it is already too privileged for the world to afford, and it must learn to live at a simpler and more disciplined level, using fewer resources.

I share with this point of view a sense of the continuing tragedy of world poverty and also a concern for the resource drain our country imposes upon our planet's raw material and energy reserves. I am persuaded, however, that only in a more equal America can our society stop its mad-dash running and so accept graciously the necessary disciplines of a more equal world. The real *middle* class in America today is living on a tight family budget that affords little in the way of extravagance. And out there in the wider society there is little to help them if they stumble or fall. The program of social reconstruction outlined here would prepare average Americans to accept a different kind of economic future from that based upon the no-holds-barred, wide-open rush of the past. With a lower ceiling on our dreams of wealth and a higher floor of socially guaranteed security and decency, our system of estimating personal worth could disengage itself from its boom-or-bust type hoping. If average Americans need no longer run so hard to lay hold of their self-respect—if nobody can really get that far ahead of anybody else or fall that far into disgrace—this would do much to drain the psychic steam out of our desperate economic rush.

The New Necessity

But more is urging toward this social reconstruction than just the allure of a more equal society. The truth is that neither the world nor we as a nation can afford any longer the explosive economic growth which has typified our nation for the past century. There is a new necessity in our future comprised of dwindling raw material reserves (especially those that can be extracted easily and cheaply), increasing costs of energy and pollution control, and a new demand on the part of the supplier nations for a larger economic return on their raw material exports. We are having to learn to live in a finite world, a world which has limits both as regards its ecology and its competing international interests.

This idea of limits is not dear to the American spirit. Speed, distance, open horizons—GOING PLACES!—they are what we admire and reward. That is what is behind our national love affair with the mobile home—as if a home could in fact be "mobile." It will not be easy for us to learn the lessons of our new, more narrow world.

This new world is so different from that once New World we knew and loved. But necessity is a fearsome teacher. And it is necessity which will bring the change. But if this change is unaccompanied by the cultivation of more appropriate virtues, it may come in a dehumanizing form—namely, as a tyranny.

What is this new necessity?

John Kyl, assistant secretary of the U.S. Department of Interior, pointed out recently: "We'll have a crisis in materials within five years.... If you list the basic minerals we use regularly," he explained, "a number of them we have to import 100 percent."[2] Put this together with the estimate of raw material reserves made by the now famous Club of Rome's report, *The Limits to Growth,*[3] and you begin to get an idea of how our new, more narrow world will look. According to the Club of Rome's computer estimate, nonrenewable natural resources like copper and aluminum, if use continues at the given rate of growth, will be exhausted in 21 and 31 years respectively. Natural gas will run out in 22 years; and even calculating a discovery of 5 times the known world reserves, it can last only 49 years. Tin will be exhausted in 15 years and lead in 21 years unless the present rate of use is sharply curtailed.

As these reserves are depleted and the cost of extracting them increases, the supplier nations in the Third World will find themselves in a situation both of new power and of new domestic need. Not only will these nations need to protect themselves against the inflated costs of imported industrial products, they will also, as in the case of the petroleum exporting countries, have a limited time to generate the capital necessary to convert their domestic economies from exclusive dependency upon their raw material exports. Even if the Club of Rome predictions prove to be overly gloomy, the prospects are high for joint action by supplier nations to increase the prices of scarce resources. While the United States, with some domestic reserves, is in a better position than Japan or Europe, we cannot in the long run protect ourselves from the effect of this continuous cost inflation in the world market.

This long-range rise in the global price of many essential resources will create an entirely new situation in world economic relations. Lester R. Brown, of the Overseas Development Council, sees this. "The shift from traditional buyers' market to global sellers' market for a lengthening list of commodities," he says, "is bringing a host of far-reaching changes, many of which are still only remotely sensed."[4] Moreover, this shift coincides with the arrival of many new "middle-class" countries—Mexico, Brazil, Venezuela, Poland, East Germany, the Soviet Union, and now the capital-rich Arab oil nations. The market for the furnishings of the Good Life is growing rapidly more competitive, and so more expensive.

What all this adds up to is that in the future it will cost the United States a lot more just to keep the Gross National Product at the level it presently has achieved—to say nothing of rapidly expanding it. The days of our rapid economic growth are over. And that means that the social myths which that kind of economy made possible are also over. As the economic pie gets no larger, the question of the fairness of the way it gets sliced up (the income/wealth distribution) becomes ever more obvious and urgent. *The dream which has disguised the steep inequality in America is ending.*

Some social interpreters who see this coming—an example is economist Robert Heilbroner—forecast the rise of tyrannical rule in most industrial nations as they wrestle with their mounting domestic difficulties.[5] Traditional politics, such critics feel, will simply collapse under the strain of the new necessity. I disagree. It seems to me there is a politics, one of majoritarian consent, which is becoming available within this new situation. It is the politics of equality. It would be based upon a broad, middle- and lower-class coalition. It would be centered upon the task of revising our tax and estate laws and our patterns of corporate ownership, in order to supply with these new revenues a higher floor of socially guaranteed decency—in medical and dental care, in education, food, and housing, and in the control of environmental degradation.

The vision which can fuel this new politics is the vision of a *fairer America,* where a person does not need to run so hard to win respect, an America where we can find fulfillment in the place *where we are* rather than the place we dream we someday might reach. The virtues cultivated by such a society would be the virtues of householding, sharing both the blessings and the burdens—*mutual shelter*—rather than running against each other in the race to grab advantages. With a shorter distance between winners and losers, we might turn our national energies to more generous talents than those encouraged by the stampede for status and success in a competitive society.

Society has always been much more than a marketplace that distributes winners and losers, although we have not been helped by the style of our everyday living to notice it. Society has always been the place where we decide what kind of people we want to be. We would be a better kind of people if a changed society could come about.

A Politics of Equality

What we are talking about here is a possibility, a *potential* new politics. There is little assurance that it will come to pass. But because the potential is *real,* and because so many good people have pretty nearly given up on politics, it is something important to explore.

Any program which aims at helping the middle class that does not at the same moment speak of a redistribution of income and wealth has, as its *concrete effect,* simply steepened the present inequalities. An example is the recent revision of college scholarship and loan guidelines to include previously ineligible middle-income families. Because the total money available was not simultaneously enlarged, it simply meant shifting the focus of benefits away from the poor— especially black and Hispanic students—to those immediately above them on the ladder of survival.

A politics of equality —if it is to be about equality in practice rather than in rhetoric—must aim at sharply increasing the level of public funding to help in the education, health care, housing, and environmental quality of the life of lower and middle classes. This money *is available.* It can be attained by closing those tax loopholes which now benefit in any significant way only the rich. Such loopholes are the special capital gains rate, gift and charitable deductions, tax-free state and municipal bonds, the depletion and depreciation allowances, and tax advantages from certain kinds of business and farm "losses."

To take one example, economists Joseph Pechman and Benjamin Okner suggest a "no-loophole system." Each family would be allowed a $2,000 standard deduction, plus the $750 personal exemption for each member, and the tax would then be figured on the resulting base without further adjustment. If one wanted simply to maintain the present level of federal revenues, the tax rate on that base could be *reduced* from the present 14 to 70 percent to a new 8 to 40 percent range.

However, our purpose is not simply to close loopholes but to generate new revenue. The top rate should be sharply higher than the 40 percent suggested by Pechman and Okner—perhaps as high as 90 percent on incomes in excess of $100,000. Such a rate schedule would both sharply increase federal revenues and sharply decrease the degree of inequality in our income structure.[6]

Beyond the revision of income tax laws, funds for raising the floor of socially guaranteed decency can be generated by steeply reducing the size of the estate one is permitted to leave one's heirs. Great Britain is already actively taking hold of this issue—namely, the issue of family fortunes that continue over the generations and freeze significant wealth at the top of society. The estate size mentioned prominently by the British Labor government is $245,000. Beyond this figure, absolute confiscation would take hold. Where precisely to draw the line for our own country—at $245,000 or nearer the $800,000 suggested by Senator McGovern in his 1972 presidential race—needs more careful study than we can undertake here. Our point is simply that such a line *needs to be drawn.*

Immediately cries will arise about the good done by wealthy families operating through foundations in subsidizing the arts, private colleges, scientific and social research, and other similiar endeavors. These are real benefits to our nation and should not be lightly passed off. One way to preserve these benefits might be to make the foundations into public corporations. This would allow the charitable work of the foundations to continue, while closing them off as sources of disguised family benefit and business control. Moreover, it would have the salutory effect of separating genuinely philanthropic purposes from those that have no socially generous goal.

Under circumstances of sharply reduced charitable deductions and estate size maximum, no doubt much of the funding of the arts, private schools and colleges, and so on would need to be picked up by various public agencies. Still, it is the public in part which is *already financing* these causes by granting special tax exemptions—which must be made up by the average taxpayer. It seems only fair that these funding decisions should be made politically (i.e., publicly) accountable. Freedom is not lost thereby but enhanced, except, of course, the freedom of certain wealthy persons to underwrite those causes and institutions which meet their own special tastes and/or interests.

But our purposes are not simply to find new funds through tax and estate law modifications, although that is an important task, so that the middle is not improved just by further pushing down the poor. Our purpose is also an equality that enhances dignity. It is a greater equalizing of relative social status in order to take some of the emulative panic and pain out of our society.

We posed this issue earlier when we asked what happens to a person's self-estimate when he or she works in a firm where the top executive makes fifty or even one hundred times as much as that firm's lowest paid employee. We raised this issue again when speaking of the way financial reward is allocated in our society so as to squeeze-off many kinds of career choices. For example, the decision to become a school teacher or a playground director—jobs which are of direct benefit to the immediate community—should not be burdened with the prospect of having to have both husband and wife work most of their married years just to attain a decent level of living for the family.

As there needs to be a redistribution of income and wealth, so also there needs to be a more careful, a more humanly enriching and freeing way of assigning wage differentials. At present the "market" operates in an irrational and demeaning way. It prevents many from undertaking types of work they most desire, types of work which may be highly beneficial to the neighborhood.

What we are talking about is the entrance of society and of rational social planning into areas we have been taught to think of as purely private—salary negotiations between owners and employees. In fact, this line between the private and the social sectors has long since become fuzzy. Special tax breaks (that is, social policy) which are available to corporations have long since modified the way in which executive remuneration takes place in large firms—supplementing salary with plush business expense allowances, yearly or semiyearly business and educational meetings at exotic island resorts, company-owned cars and airplanes, and various stock option plans which can be paid for by internal company loans at low interest rates.

Indeed, this whole area is already so saturated with public policy that one suspects that much of the hue and cry detonated whenever one mentions revising remuneration differentials has little to do with fear of losing individual freedom and much to do with the prospect of losing the special benefits available to the special few. As in the case of foundations, here, too, the proposed modifications will operate to *open up* society and so enhance individual freedom for the vast majority.

Furthermore, I would suggest modifying through public legislation the income pyramids, so that a particular position of executive responsibility would receive, let us say, *no more than ten times the salary of the firm's lowest paid employee.* This would allow for plenty of incentive, but divert the energy we now spend on envy and obsequiousness into humanly more ennobling tasks. It is the great virtue of economist John Kenneth Galbraith that he sees the importance of this salary differential question. "Once the planning system [his phrase for the system of large corporations] is stripped of its market disguise," Galbraith points out,

> the way it arranges its compensation becomes a question of much interest and the proper subject of public policy. The differential that is set between those who get the most and those who get the least requires justification. And the conclusion that these differentials reflect an egregious and indefensible inequality becomes inescapable.[7]

Not only should sharp limits be set upon wage differentials, but also public policy should act to open up previously poorly rewarded jobs to parallel wage accomplishment. The most expert and efficient car repairmen and the most care-taking of day-care teachers should have incomes equal to those of the proven leaders of business or law. There should be a *demonopolization* of top-pay type work through the social creation of multiple income peaks available throughout *the whole spectrum of socially useful work.*

At this point I can hear someone exclaiming that I should *stop dreaming and start being practical!* Still, this whole book has been nothing but an extended exercise in being practical. It has studied closely the style in our society of our everyday practice. It is this practical course of analysis which has led us to this preliminary puzzling through how we might go about making our country a more ennobling place to live.

Having begun that task by an analysis of income and wealth distribution, and asking what changes might enhance our quality of life, we come now to a second difficulty. On face, the economic changes I have suggested would seem to increase sharply the concentration of power in federal govern ment. We need remember, however, how much of this concentration has already taken place behind the false claims of free enterprise. The reforms suggested here would have the effect of *nationalizing* th old-boy network and special-interest system, and making then into fully public and politically accountable processes of social planning.

But it is important that there also be a sharply decentralized system of public planning and funding units, right down to the local community level. The present Federal Revenue Sharing Program is a step in this direction, but only a small one. Its full potential awaits a new vision of a more neighborhood-oriented society. Decisions should be made at the local community level as to the allocation of public resources which affect that area. What such a decentralized society might look like and what some of the problems encountered would be we turn to next.

Decentralization

Governor Tom Judge of Montana recently launched into a contest which, until a few years ago, would have been unthinkable. He sharply challenged the truthfulness of *both* Exxon President Randall Meyer *and* the U.S. Department of the Interior concerning their plans for coal and oil development in his state. His challenge reflects a growing awareness that local communities must defend themselves not only against vested business interests but also against the vested friends of business in the federal government. "It is important," Governor Judge said, "that Western states work together in energy development; otherwise we'll get ripped off one at a time. We have to present a strong front to the Government and energy companies."[8]

This sense of the need for local community and regional self-defense is rapidly spreading. Whether it is communities fighting housing industry interests and their all-too-willing friends in City Hall against the ruin imposed by a too rapid influx of new residents into a given area, or consumer and elderly groups fighting the utility companies and their friends on the state Public Utility Commission against steep rate hikes, or local housewives joining together to protest price gouging on dairy products where the industry has bought its way to special care in State House and White House—all these illustrate a new, more sophisticated mood. And that is based on the recognition that *the grass roots usually get trampled in the rush for the big buck.*

Breaking up the buddy system between organized interests and those government officials whose elections, plane rides, cars, "educational" trips to Miami, etc., they pay for is part of the goal of redistributing our country's wealth. Public financing of all elections—congressional, state, and municipal as well as presidential—and full financial disclosure laws will also help redemocratize our democracy. But what is finally needed is a sharp increase in the positive power of local neighborhoods operating in their own interest and defense. And that means getting tax revenues flowing into the hands of neighborhood planning groups. After all, we reside in a nation only in part, in a state only in part, and in a city only in part. A major portion of our actual everyday dwelling is done in neighborhoods—in local schools, on local streets, in local stores and professional services. To be sure, there are immense jurisdictional problems to be worked out between these various sectors of our everyday dependencies. We do in essential ways also live in cities, states, and nations as well as neighborhoods. But just this is the point of our argument. This relationship of planning and power needs to be worked out, *self-consciously negotiated,* not simply planned from above and passed down.

What we are talking about is the reversal of our trend toward hierarchy and centralization that reduces individual responsibility and increases a person's sense of helplessness and passivity. Gar Alperovitz, a Fellow of the Institute for Policy Studies, puts the question plainly. "Could society," he asks, "ever be organized equitably, cooperatively, humanely, so wealth benefited everyone— without generating a highly centralized, authoritarian system?"[9] This question—whether equality can be coordinated with a pluralism of power and diverse sources of individual initiative—is central to our vision of a better America. Our wager is that the answer can be "yes."

Individual responsibility, voluntary cooperation, and reciprocal obligation on a face-to-face basis, in the final analysis, are the only protection against the bureaucratic-hierarchical mode of social organization. Political scientist Robert Dahl has worked on these issues at the level of worker participation in the management of industry. [10] But it is difficult to see how this, by itself, would issue in anything more than a kind of "worker's capitalism," where each factory or industry would develop into a special interest group lobbying against the broader community. Dahl foresees some of these issues and looks to interest group representation in a more widely based planning unit that could jointly work out factory and community interests. This planning unit would need to include representatives of all the community's constituent members—minorities, service workers, housewives, youth, and the elderly—and not just industrial workers.

But this proposal still leaves a host of issues that cannot be dealt with locally, or on a day-by-day basis. Neighborhoods, after all, are connected by their power lines, gas mains, trolley car and railroad tracks to other neighborhoods and linked together with them into city and regional systems of interaction and dependency. Gar Alperovitz sees the problems here and offers, it seems to me, a viable vision for the future. "The locality," he says, "should be conceived as *a basis for* (not an alternative to) a larger framework of regional and national coordinating institutions." [11]

William Appleman Williams and Robert Lafont have taken up this notion and developed it in the direction of a "Commonwealth of Regions," where the association would be at the level of intermediate units "larger than a 'community' but smaller than a nation of 300 million people." [12] These regional units would take over the general oversight of the capital and productive functions, which are now controlled by the five hundred largest corporations, banks and insurance companies, within their geographic area—business firms whose previously internal decisions had region-wide effect and so should be made publicly accountable. The Tennessee Valley Authority provides a suggestive precedent for such regional control and planning. [13]

All of this would still leave many of the essential coordinating factors to the federal government—national defense and general tax policy being but two of the more obvious. Still, the rule here should be to leave as much planning and funding control as possible to the localities where people actually reside and work, elevating only those issues which absolutely must be worked out at a higher regional or national level. Moreover, the very dynamics of a slowed economic growth rate, which we have foreseen in any case, will aid in this process of maximum localization, for the problems of adequate planning will become more stable and predictable than in the earlier buccaneer stage of growth.

It is perfectly clear that what I have been urging in this decentralization and the previous "wealth" sections of this chapter *raise more questions than they answer*. But it is also clear that these questions must be raised, studied, and eventually acted upon if democracy in our country is to have a future. The intent here is simply to point the direction of the needed changes.

There are, on the other hand, many already pointing in the opposite direction—toward ever-increasing centralization, bureaucratic hierarchy and control, and eventually even tyranny. As our world—both social and natural—becomes more narrow (in terms of energy and raw material costs as well as scarcities, environmental degradation pressures, and frustrated middle-class hopes), the choice will be thrust upon us. And one way or another, we will decide. I want that decision to go one way rather than the other; and I believe most of the readers will, too. That is why—however vaguely and without full anticipation of the problems—we need to begin now to discuss the general direction of our common social future. Equalization and decentralization, I think, point the way toward the preservation of our democratic freedoms.

These two elements will likely come in successive steps. First, the move toward a more equal society will be initiated by changing the tax and estate laws. When combined with public financing of elections and strengthened disclosure laws, this change will help to politicize and open up the big money/organized-interest-group system of public favor and make our society more fair. The second step, decentralization, will likely come not so much as an overall program as a direction and pressure of policy. Decentralization needs to take root in the local community, rather than being imposed from above. There will probably be a rather lengthy process of trial and error as the various units compose themselves, undertake an expanding web of projects, and, together with the larger units of region and nation, work out their respective systems of representation, planning coordination, and accountability.

Still, for all the tentativeness and difficulty of this decentralizing process, we should remember that we are not simply whistling in the dark here. Already community corporations are being experimented with successfully. Community development groups like FIGHT in Rochester, New York, are now operating community-owned electrical manufacturing plants of considerable size. In Los Angeles, Operation Bootstrap has established a community toy factory, and in Cleveland there is a collectively run rubber molding factory. In Philadelphia a large community-owned shopping center is located close to the campus of Temple University.[14]

These are the community models which prefigure a future society of democratic decentralization, where wealth is more equitably distributed without simply fueling a centralized state socialism that has no way of instructing persons in the art of self-government and a sense of individual competence for living. This nurture of self-esteem, I believe, will mark the direction of democracy in the years to come. People remain free only as long as they believe in themselves and so demand freedom.

Household and Home

After several weeks of discussing the issues examined in this book, an undergraduate approached me after class. She announced that the course had been a success because she felt "guilty" and knew that I was "right." She was, it turned out, from a family of considerable wealth. I took the opportunity to talk with the class about why guilt—just as animosity—was a misplaced response to this study. It is not persons we have been analyzing, but processes. The issue is not the virtue, or the lack of it, of wealthy people. There is much of each there; even as there is much of each among the poor and middle classes. Rather the issue is structural—the system of gaining and keeping inordinate advantage and what it does to our country's quality of life.

This seems an important thing to say in a book such as this, which lays heavy stress upon the interaction of economic and psychological processes in America. My purpose has been to outline a more generous nation, not a more angry one, where the virtues of householding might take easier and firmer hold. And as in any household, greater fairness produces more health. What makes a home a good home is the sense of equal belonging.

The arts of householding encourage an opposite wisdom from that cleverness which handles problems by avoiding them or deflecting them to impact upon others as we move safely out from under. Householding begins with *a sense of limits,* of a defined space within which we live and so need jointly to maintain as livable. The virtues of dwelling take root in a sense of place and common belonging.

To be sure, we need the allure of horizons, the freedom of new distances to explore. But it is essential, too, for us to have a belonging-place to come home to, especially when horizons disappear into the darkness of night. Indeed, one of the truly significant events in the evolution of the human spirit—probably the only one in our generation—can be associated with the first flight to the moon. It opened up a new perspective upon our precarious spaceship earth. We humankind—who alone, it seems, upon this planet puzzle about why we should be so bound—meditate upon ourselves in the picture of our homeland earth, that shrouded and distant bright blue agate, standing out against the mantle of billions of other sun systems like our own in just our galaxy. And beyond our galaxy we now know, although twenty years ago even astronomers thought just our galaxy marked the edges of the abyss, are billions of other galaxies each with its billions of sun systems. Billions raised to the billionth power—you can see how it makes us feel a bit lonely.

In a curious way, we watch ourselves as we watch stars being born, incubated in the clouds of the Horsehead nebulae. We contemplate our planet's end, as we see those experiments in being which have not yet fully come into being, whose suns have not focused and formed themselves out of the swirling hydrogen clouds, and whose destinies lie beyond the destiny of our solar system's demise. And suddenly— yes, suddenly, indeed, in terms of the evolution of the human spirit— this earthland home of ours is no longer taken for granted in that so innocent bravado of the traveler who desires only unaccomplished quests and ignores the place he stands upon. We have a new sense of household and home.

We have, we know, this one fragile dwelling. Thus, when systems failed, we watched in fascination our companions, with all the miracles of technology around them, frantically clawing their way back to earth and home and safety, jury-rigging collapsing substitutes to evacuate their dying air, in that omen sent from space called Apollo 13. A telling moment in the career of the modern spirit! Transcendence can never hereafter—except as a kind of profound forgetfulness—move just outward toward God the Father without pondering also that hovering, protective mantle of earth from which continuingly humankind takes its birth and returns in death.

"Household and Home"—the vision of a different future and a different and better and fairer society in a more equal world—these are our new challenges, indeed our *new necessities*. They await our courage of spirit to grasp them with hope and care, and make them real.

NOTES

Chapter 1

[1] C. Wright Mills, "The Power Elite: Comment on Criticism," *Dissent,* Winter, 1957.

[2] "A Closer Look at the Middle Class," *U.S. News and World Report,* October 14, 1974, p. 45.

[3] *Confidence and Concern: Citizens View American Government,* Harris Poll, September, 1973.

[4] Lee Soltow, ed., *Six Papers on the Size Distribution of Wealth and Income* (New York: National Bureau of Economic Research, Inc., 1969), p. 122.

[5] James Kuhn, "Money—Who Is Taxed? For Whom?" in *The Columbia Forum,* Spring, 1973, p. 45.

[6] Philip M. Stern, *The Rape of the Taxpayer* (New York: Random House, Inc., 1973), p. 116.

[7] See Willard R. Johnson, "Should the Poor Buy No Growth?" in *Daedalus,* Fall, 1973, p. 188, fn. 35.

[8] *Ibid.,* p. 177.

[9] *Ibid.,* p. 176.

[10] Peter Barnes, "The GNP Machine," *The New Republic,* September 30, 1972, p. 19.

[11] Stern, *op. cit.,* p. 11.

[12] Richard Sennett and Jonathan Cobb, *The Hidden Injuries of Class* (New York: Alfred A. Knopf, Inc., 1972), *passim.*

[13] As quoted in Moses Rischin, ed., *The American Gospel of Success* (Chicago: Quadrangle Books, Inc., 1965), p. 45.

[14] Sennett and Cobb, *op. cit.,* pp. 221-224.

[15]Quoted in Donald Meyer, *The Positive Thinkers* (Garden City: Doubleday & Company, Inc., 1965), p. 260.

[16]*Ibid.,* p. 263.

[17]From Richard Parker, *The Myth of the Middle Class* (New York: Liveright, 1972), p. 6, with permission of publisher. Copyright © 1972 Richard Parker.

[18]*Ibid.,* p. 132.

Chapter 2

[1]See "And Now a Word from Mr. & Mrs. Middle," *New York Times,* "News of the Week in Review," July 23, 1972.

[2]*Ibid.*

[3]As reported in the *Philadelphia Inquirer,* March 2, 1974, p. 4B.

[4]"Deflating Middle Incomes," *New York Times,* "News of the Week in Review," March 24, 1974, section 3, p. 5.

[5]For a more extended discussion of the role of this "sense of fairness" in modern America, see Henry Reuss, "A Democrat's Critique of Nixonomics," *New York Times,* Magazine section, July 7, 1974.

[6]G. L. Bach, *The New Inflation* (Providence: Brown University Press, 1972), p. 3. Italics added. © 1958, 1972 by Brown University.

[7]Richard Parker, *The Myth of the Middle Class* (New York: Liveright, 1972), p. 140.

[8]*Ibid.,* p. 179.

[9]See Philip Stern, *The Rape of the Taxpayer* (New York: Random House, Inc., 1973), p. 24.

[10]Taken from James A. Maxwell, *Financing State and Local Governments* (Washington, D.C.: The Brookings Institution, 1965), Table 4-9, p. 99.

[11]Stern, *op. cit.,* p. 208.

[12]Morton Mintz and Jerry S. Cohen, *America, Inc.* (New York: The Dial Press, 1971), p. 43. Copyright © 1971 by Jerry S. Cohen and Morton Mintz. Used with permission of Dial Press.

[13]*Ibid.,* p. 45.

[14]Thorstein Veblen, *The Theory of the Leisure Class* (New York: The Modern Library, 1934), pp. 22-26.

[15]*Ibid.,* pₗ. 30-31.

[16]*Ibid.,* pp. 68-88.

[17]Arthur Miller, *Death of a Salesman* (New York: The Viking Press, Inc., 1949), p. 138. Copyright 1949 by Arthur Miller. Reprinted by permission of Viking Press, Inc.

[18]Bach, *op. cit.,* p. 65.

[19] *Ibid.,* p. 74.

[20] *Ibid.,* p. 80.

[21] Parker, *op. cit.,* p. 134.

[22] Quoted in *ibid.,* p. 137. Italics added.

[23] *Ibid.,* p. 141. Quotes Arthur Shostak, *Blue-Collar Life* (New York: Random House, Inc., 1969), p. 29.

[24] "Most U.S. Incomes Found Inadequate," *New York Times,* November 18, 1968, p. 38.

[25] *Philadelphia Inquirer,* October 14, 1974, p. 2-A.

[26] Alfred L. Malabre, Jr., "Real Bogeyman," *Wall Street Journal,* December 11, 1973, p. 1.

[27] *Ibid.*

[28] "Middle Class Personal Debts Rising in U.S. Because of Inflation," *Chicago Tribune,* July 30, 1974, p. 12.

[29] This statistic and those to follow are taken from Anne Draper, "The Price Squeeze on Living Standards," *The American Federationist,* July, 1974, p. 6.

[30] *Ibid.*

[31] *Ibid.*

[32] Don R. Conlan, "Gauging the True Growth of Profitability," *New York Times,* August 4, 1974, section 3, p. 1.

[33] Quoted in Parker, *op. cit.,* p. 178.

Chapter 3

[1] As quoted in Richard Parker, *The Myth of the Middle Class* (New York: Liveright, 1972), p. 61.

[2] For statistics, see Philip M. Stern, *The Rape of the Taxpayer* (New York: Random House, Inc., 1973), p. 9 and Parker, *op. cit.,* p. 178.

[3] See Stern, *op. cit.,* p. 325.

[4] *Ibid.,* p. 323.

[5] *Ibid.,* p. 28.

[6] The statistics on family foundations and the facts in the following two paragraphs are taken from Ben Whitaker, *The Philanthropoids* (New York: William Morrow Co., 1974), pp. 13 and 119-120, 125, 127.

[7] As quoted in Whitaker, *op. cit.,* p. 124.

[8] As quoted in Stern, *op. cit.,* p. 330.

[9] Quoted in Stanley S. Surrey, *Pathways to Tax Reform* (Cambridge: Harvard University Press, 1973), pp. 59-60.

[10] Stern, *op. cit.*, pp. 17-18.

[11] Surrey, *op. cit.*, p. 54.

[12] *Ibid.*, p. 91.

[13] See G. William Domhoff, *Who Rules America?* (Englewood Cliffs, N.J.: Prentice-Hall, Inc., 1967), pp. 47-50.

[14] Stern, *op. cit.*, p. 226. See also John Kenneth Galbraith, *Economics and the Public Purpose* (Boston: Houghton Mifflin Company, 1973) for a detailed exposition of the loss of market strength by smaller business firms.

[15] As quoted in Morton Mintz and Jerry S. Cohen, *America, Inc.* (New York: The Dial Press, 1971), p. 65, n. 58.

[16] Domhoff, *op. cit.*, p. 57.

[17] Mintz and Cohen, *op. cit.*, p. 75.

[18] Quoted from *ibid.*, p. xv.

[19] *Ibid.*, pp. 224-225.

[20] Stern, *op. cit.*, p. 383.

[21] Quoted in Mintz and Cohen, *op. cit.*, pp. 186-187.

[22] *Ibid.*, p. 164.

[23] As quoted in *ibid.*, p. 166.

[24] See Domhoff, *op. cit.*, p. 144.

[25] "Following the Milk Trail," *Newsweek,* July 29, 1974, pp. 32-33.

[26] Mintz and Cohen, *op. cit.*, p. 133.

[27] Suzanne Keller, *Beyond the Ruling Class* (New York: Random House, Inc., 1963), p. 264.

[28] As quoted in Peter Bachrach, *The Theory of Democratic Elitism* (Boston: Little, Brown and Company, 1967), p. 74.

[29] Quoted in Galbraith, *op. cit.*, p. 81.

[30] Daniel Bell, *The Coming of Post-Industrial Society* (New York: Basic Books, Inc., 1973), p. 344. Copyright © 1973 by Daniel Bell.

[31] This thesis is discussed by William Kornhauser in his *The Politics of Mass Society* (New York: The Free Press, 1959), *passim.* Keller also holds this view.

[32] Keller, *op. cit.*, p. 265.

[33] Bell, *op. cit.*, p. 34.

[34] As quoted in Bachrach, *op. cit.,* p. 60, n. 39.

[35] E. E. Schattschneider, *The Semisovereign People* (New York: Holt, Rinehart and Winston, 1960), p. 35.

[36] Bachrach, *op. cit.,* p. 37. Copyright © 1967, Little, Brown and Company, Inc. Reprinted by permission.

[37] *Ibid.,* p. 2.

Chapter 4

[1] Quoted in Suzanne Keller, *Beyond the Ruling Class* (New York: Random House, Inc., 1963), p. 269.

[2] See "Introduction" and "Part 1" of Richard Sennett and Jonathan Cobb, *The Hidden Injuries of Class* (New York: Alfred A. Knopf, Inc., 1972).

[3] *Ibid.,* p. 65.

[4] G. William Domhoff, *Who Rules America?* (Englewood Cliffs, N.J.: Prentice Hall, Inc., 1967), p. 17.

[5] *Ibid.*

[6] Robert Diamond, "A Self-Portrait of the Chief Executive," *Fortune,* May, 1970, and Richard Parker, *The Myth of Middle Class* (New York: Liveright, 1972), p. 128.

[7] Domhoff, *op. cit.,* p. 18.

[8] *Ibid.,* p. 5.

[9] *Fortune, op. cit.,* p. 323.

[10] Richard Parker, *op. cit.,* p. 128.

[11] Thorstein Veblen, *The Theory of the Leisure Class* (New York: The Modern Library, 1934), p. 49.

[12] E. Digby Baltzell, *The Protestant Establishment* (New York: Random House, Inc., 1964).

[13] *Ibid.,* p. 208.

[14] *Ibid.,* p. 349.

[15] *Time,* July 2, 1965, p. 47.

[16] Michael Novak, *The Rise of the Unmeltable Ethnics* (New York: The Macmillan Company, 1972), p. 213.

[17] Quoted in Baltzell, *op. cit.,* p. 221.

[18] John H. Schaar, "Equality of Opportunity and Beyond," in *Up the Mainstream,* ed. Herbert G. Reid (New York: David McKay Co., Inc., 1974), p. 241.

[19] Alexis de Tocqueville, *Democracy in America* (New York: Alfred A. Knopf, Inc., 1945), vol. 2, pp. 136-137.

[20] See Garry Wills, *Nixon Agonistes* (Boston: Houghton Mifflin Company, 1970), *passim.*

[21] Schaar, *op. cit.,* pp. 234-235.

[22] *Ibid.,* p. 238.

[23] *Ibid.,* p. 245.

Chapter 5

[1] As quoted in Reinhold Niebuhr, *The Irony of American History* (New York: Charles Scribner's Sons, 1952), p. 51.

[2] Russell H. Conwell, "Acres of Diamonds," special printing by Temple University, 1974, p. 30, italics added.

[3] Russell H. Conwell, *Acres of Diamonds* (New York: Harper & Row, Publishers, 1915), p. 21.

[4] Conwell (pamphlet), *op. cit.,* pp. 26-27.

[5] See Max Weber, *The Protestant Ethic and the Spirit of Capitalism,* trans. Talcott Parsons (New York: Charles Scribner's Sons, 1958).

[6] Conwell (pamphlet), *op. cit.,* p. 37.

[7] *Ibid.,* pp. 37-38.

[8] *Psychology Today,* July, 1974, p. 89 (ad.).

[9] Donald Meyer, *The Positive Thinkers* (Garden City: Doubleday & Company, Inc., 1965), pp. 164-165.

[10] *Ibid.,* p. 165.

[11] *Ibid.,* p. 167.

[12] *Ibid.,* pp. 168-170.

[13] *Ibid.,* p. 197.

[14] Norman Vincent Peale, *Stay Alive All Your Life,* p. 252, quoted in *ibid.,* p. 268.

[15] Conwell (pamphlet), *op. cit.,* p. 38.

[16] *Ibid.,* p. 54.

[17] *Ibid.,* p. 54.

[18] Karl Marx, *Early Writings,* trans. and ed. T. B. Bottomore (New York: McGraw Hill Book Company, 1963), p. 191.

[19] R. H. Tawney, *The Acquisitive Society* (New York: Harcourt Brace Jovanovich, 1921), p. 35.

[20] Marx, *op. cit.,* p. 193.

[21] See Hugh Dalziel Duncan, "Money as a Form of Transcendence in American Life," in *Up the Mainstream,* ed. Herbert G. Reid (New York: David McKay Co., Inc., 1974), p. 115.

[22] *Ibid.,* p. 118.

[23] See Michael Harrington, *The Other America* (New York: The Macmillan Company, 1962). We should note, however, that Harrington was one of the earliest of our country's social interpreters to see this mistake and begin to attack the idea of a generalized abundance.

[24] As quoted in Andrew Levison, "The Working-Class Majority," *The New Yorker,* September 2, 1974, p. 58.

[25] *Ibid.,* p. 37.

[26] John Kenneth Galbraith, *The New Industrial State* (Boston: Houghton Mifflin Company, 1967), p. 4.

[27] Richard Parker, *The Myth of the Middle Class* (New York: Liveright, 1972), p. 33.

[28] As quoted in Peter Clecak, *Radical Paradoxes* (New York: Harper & Row, Publishers, 1973), p. 175.

[29] Levison, *op. cit.,* p. 36.

[30] Figures quoted from *Daedalus,* Fall, 1973, pp. 176, 177, note 35 on p. 188. See also Parker, *op. cit.,* p. 8.

[31] See Parker, *op. cit.,* p. 121.

[32] See Ben Wattenberg, *The Real America* (New York: Doubleday & Company, Inc., 1974). This quote is taken from the *New York Times'* review of Wattenberg's book by Seven Weisman in the "Book Review" section, September 29, 1974, p. 27.

[33] Denis A. Goulet, "The United States: A Case of Anti-Development," *Up the Mainstream,* p. 176.

[34] *Ibid.,* p. 178.

[35] *Ibid.,* p. 181.

Chapter 6

[1] Quoted in Donella Meadows *et al., The Limits to Growth* (New York: The New American Library, Inc., 1972), p. 135.

[2] Quoted from the *Philadelphia Bulletin,* September 30, 1974, p. 3B.

[3] Meadows, *op. cit.,* The charts which give the specifics referred to here can be found on pages 64-67.

[4] Quoted from Leonard Silk, "Economics 1—The Summit Chautauqua, Babel or Consensus?", *New York Times,* Sunday Magazine, Sept. 22, 1974, p. 96.

[5] See Robert Heilbroner, *An Inquiry into the Human Prospect* (New York: W. W. Norton & Company, Inc., 1974).

[6] Philip M. Stern, *The Rape of the Taxpayer* (New York: Random House, Inc., 1973). See his charts on pages 420-421. He also details the Pechman-Okner plan on page 408.

[7] John Kenneth Galbraith, *Economics and the Public Purpose* (Boston: Houghton Mifflin Company, 1973), pp. 265-266.

[8] Quoted from Winthrop Griffith, "An Eco-freak for Governor?", *New York Times,* Sunday Magazine, Oct. 27, 1974, p. 35.

[9] See Gar Alperovitz, "Notes Toward a Pluralist Commonwealth," in Staughton Lynd and Gar Alperovitz, *Strategy and Program* (Boston: Beacon Press, 1973), p. 53. I have used his ideas extensively in the next several paragraphs.

[10] See Robert A. Dahl, *After the Revolution?* (New Haven: Yale University Press, 1970).

[11] Alperovitz, *op. cit.,* p. 66. Italics added for emphasis.

[12] *Ibid.,* p. 75. See also William Appleman Williams, *The Great Evasion* (Chicago: Quadrangle Books, Inc., 1964) and Robert Lafont, *La Revolution Regionaliste* (Paris: Editions Gallimard, 1957).

[13] Alperovitz, *op. cit.,* p. 75.

[14] See "Profiles in Community-Based Economic Development," from the Cambridge Institute and the Centre for Community Economic Development, 1878 Massachusetts Ave., Cambridge, MA 02140.

INDEX